CARE AND EDUCATION OF DIFFERENTLY ABLED

About the Author

Prof. G. Pankajam, former Vice Chancellor of Gandhigram Rural University, is a post-graduate in Home Science with Child Development as her specialization from M.S. University, Baroda. She did her Ph.D. in Education from Madurai Kamaraj University and M.Ed. from S.N.D.T. Women's University, Mumbai.

Prof. Pankajam has four decades of teaching, research and administrative experience. She has authored and edited more than 25 books and presented and published about 150 papers. She has also designed curriculum for under-graduate, diploma and post-graduate programmes in Home Science, Pre-Primary Education, Child Development and Education for different universities and NCERT as an expert of National Curriculum Framework Committee. She has prepared Learning Modules for Child Development, Pre-Primary Education, Challenges in Education, Extension Education and Guidance and Counselling for distance education programme of many universities.

CARE AND EDUCATION OF DIFFERENTLY ABLED

G. Pankajam

CONCEPT PUBLISHING COMPANY, NEW DELHI-110 059

Cataloging in Publication Data—DK
Courtesy: D.K. Agencies (P) Ltd. <docinfo@dkagencies.com>

Pankajam, G. (Gnanasundaram), 1939-
Care and education of differently abled / G. Pankajam.
p. cm.
In Indian context.
Includes bibliographical references (p.).
Includes index.
ISBN 13: 9788180695773
ISBN 10: 8180695778

1. Children with disabilities—India. 2. Children with disabilities—Care—India. 3. Children with disabilities—Education—India. 4. Children with disabilities—Rehabilitation—India. I. Title.

DDC 362.408 309 54 22

ISBN-13: 978-81-8069-577-3 (HB)
ISBN-10: 81-8069-577-8 (HB)

First Published 2009

Published and Printed by
Ashok Kumar Mittal
Concept Publishing Company
A/15-16, Commercial Block, Mohan Garden
New Delhi-110 059 (INDIA)

Phones : 25351460, 25351794
Fax : 091-11-25357103
Email : publishing@conceptpub.com

Preface

"Flower Without One Petal is Still a Flower."

People with disabilities were not very visible during the past. We know that they were there, but we do not know much about them. It was often felt that the best option for disabled people was to be placed in an institution. Many people have tried to hide people with disabilities. Parents of children with a disability were sometimes told: "Place your child in an institution, forget it and try to have another child!" Many did so, in spite of their unwillingness and with lot of pain for themselves and even more so for the child.

The First and Second World War changed the perception of disability. Many people became disabled as a result of the wars and resources were spent on providing care for the disabled young and old. The society and the government thought that it was their responsibility to take care of them and to provide job opportunities for which they are capable.

Care, education and rehabilitation of the disabled like visually impaired, hearing impaired, physical and health impairment, mentally challenged, gifted etc. is a difficult and challenging task to parents, teachers and the public. They need to have patience, interest, and commitment, understand their needs and know-how of different types of disabilities. We should accept that the disabled too have the right to proper care, education, recreation, vocation and a normal family life. They do not want to be treated differently.

"Education for All" includes education of disabled also either by providing special or integrated education. This is a progressive and positive action towards achieving the goal of normalization by providing equal opportunity to the disabled also. This will be successful only when the community accepts integrating the disabled in the normal school, positively. In India the integrated education is still in its infant stage. Parents, teachers and the public would still prefer special schools only for the disabled children and not to mingle with normal children.

According to the United Nations there are 600 million people with a disability in the world, a figure which is based on the assumption that 10 per cent of the world's population has a disability. While most developing countries report 3-7 per cent incidence of disability and the industrialized countries report 15-25 per cent. The difference, of course, depends on how they define disability. Disability is no longer seen as merely a result of impairment. It is a fact that nearly 70 per cent of the disabilities are preventable. It is estimated that among the disabled only 0.2 per cent have access to rehabilitation services as 80 per cent of the disabled live in rural area where the rehabilitation services are not available.

If we assume that 15 per cent of the world's population is people with disabilities we are talking of 900 million people in this book. That will be the world's largest minority. Only China and India would have a population larger than the number of people with disabilities in the world. It is believed that four out of five people with disabilities in the world live in the Asia Pacific region, many of them in poverty and under miserable living conditions.

In the late 60s and 70s people with disabilities, inspired by the civil rights and women's right movements, started demanding their rights. The declaration of a UN international year of disabled people in 1981 was the beginning of a new international era in the disability movement, as it sent a strong and important message to the world.

People with disabilities are being discriminated against in all societies all over the world. We have designed and constructed our societies, as though persons with disabilities did not exist, as if all human being can walk, hear, see, and understand complex messages from people around them. Discrimination is often unintentional and indirect. For example, when someone with a disability wants to study a certain career, that person might be advised to choose another career because the university is inaccessible due to her/his disability, rather that particular course was not designed to suit that particular disability.

Providing rehabilitation should become the responsibility of the community, as it is easier, economical and meaningful to take care of the disabled at their doorstep than taking them out to an unknown place. Rehabilitation means returning to or coming back as much as possible to the life before the accident or disease that caused the disability. It is defined in the Standard Rules as "a process aimed at enabling persons with disabilities to reach and maintain their optimal physical, sensory and/or social functional levels, thus providing them with the tools to change their lives towards a higher level of independence." Rehabilitation is now viewed as a process in which people with disabilities and their advocates make decisions about what services they need to enhance their participation.

Professionals who provide rehabilitation services have the responsibility to give relevant information to people with disabilities so that they can make informed decisions regarding what is appropriate for them. The term rehabilitation describes the wide range of ways used to assist in enabling persons who are born with disabilities. Their needs are often different from the needs of people who acquire disabilities through, for example, an accident or a disease. Rehabilitation means to restore a condition, operation or capacity.

The UN Charter also says, "Community Based Rehabilitation should be widely promoted nationally and internationally as an affordable and sustainable approach to services," particularly in developing countries like India as this method involves people participation directly in the rehabilitation programme.

For many people with disabilities assistive technology is a favourable condition for participating in society freely, going to school, having a job, meeting friends, playing sports or participating in cultural activities. Today assistive technology can mean so many different things from a wheelchair, to a hearing aid, to synthetic speech on a computer for a blind person. Assistive technology was defined in a study funded by the European Union called HEART—Horizontal European Activities in Rehabilitation Technology—as "any product, instrument, equipment or technical system used by people with disabilities and older people—specially produced or generally available—to prevent, compensate, relieve or neutralize the disability and to improve the individual's autonomy and quality of life." It need not be a mechanized instrument. Even a White Cane—the third eye to a visually challenged which makes him/her mobile is an assistive instrument.

Parents, teachers, students and the public should understand and realize that they have the responsibility of taking care of the disabled and treat them as their equals in every respect without any discrimination. Infact disability in one dimension need not curtail other activities. They are differently abled in other functioning, even excel the normal people in that activity. I realized this when I was a student of Human Development/Child Development and visited many institutions for disabled in different parts of the country. I taught the course at the teacher education and postgraduate levels in India and in USA as a Fulbright Scholar. I had the opportunity to guide the M.Phil and Ph.D. scholars who had taken problems relating to differently abled children for their Research.

As a member of National Standing Committee of CAPART, Ministry of Rural Development, Government of India, I had the opportunity to understand the problems and issues relating to the disabled and the efforts taken by NGOs to provide rehabilitation services at the community itself with the assistance of CAPART. This Community Based Rehabilitation (CBR) seems to be effective and successful in many places especially in rural area where there are nearly 80 per cent of the uncared disabled live.

All these experiences I had, induced and motivated me to write this book entitled *"Care and Education of Differently Abled"*. I will be happy if all those who read this book get inspired and feel that they too have the responsibility to care for their unfortunate brothers and sisters and empower them to compete with normal people to lead a normal life. They don't need our sympathy. They want the opportunities to develop their other skills so that they can be independent and contribute to the national development like their counterparts.

I thank the administrative staff of Kasturba Sevika Ashram who typed the manuscript. I acknowledge with thanks Dr. S. Lakshmi, Professor of English, Gandhigram Rural University, who was kind enough to read through the manuscript and make corrections. I am grateful to Mrs. Krishnaveni, Prinipal, Shanthi School for the Deaf, Sivasailam and her husband Sri Ganesan for helping me to get the photographs from different schools for differently abled children. My thanks are due to my family members who gave me moral support while I was writing the book.

The book in this form was made possible because of Concept Publishing Company. I sincerely thank M/s. Concept Publishing Company, New Delhi who has willingly come forward to publish the book.

I remember with gratitude late Dr. K.P. Kala, Principal, Annammal College of Education, Tuticorin who helped me a lot when I started writing this book.

Gandhigram **G. Pankajam**

Contents

Preface 5

1. Children with Special Needs **15**
- Introduction 15
- Children with Special Needs—Definitions and Classification 16
- Efforts taken to Solve/Combat the Problems of Children with Special Needs 18
- Education and Care of Children with Special Needs 19
- Inclusive Education 22
- Effective Special Education Programme 23
- Review Questions 25

2. Physical and Health Impairment **26**
- Learning Objectives 26
- Definition 27
- Types of Orthopaedic/Physical Disabilities 27
- Identification of Orthopaedically Handicapped/ Physically Impaired 30
- Educational Provisions 30
- Review Questions 36

3. Sensory Disabilities **37**
- Learning Objectives 37
- **I. Visually Impaired** **38**
  - Classification 39
  - Identification of Visually Impaired 40
  - Causes of Visual Impairment 41
  - Characteristics and Problems of Visually Impaired 42
  - Educational Provisions 46
  - Prevention 48

II. Speech Disorders	**49**
Definitions	50
Causes of Speech Impairment	50
Problems of Speech Impairment	52
Education Provisions	52
III. Hearing Impairment	**55**
Definition	55
Causes of Hearing Impairment	59
Characteristics of Hearing Impaired	60
Identification of Hearing Impaired	61
Educational Provisions for Hearing Impaired	62
Review Questions	63
4. Mentally Challenged	**65**
Classification of Mentally Challenged Children	68
Causes of Mental Retardation	72
Characteristics of Mentally Retarded	75
Identification of Mentally Challenged Children	77
Educating the Mentally Challenged	77
1. Curriculum for Dependent Mentally Challenged	78
Types of Special Education Programme	79
2. Education of the Educable Mentally Challenged	79
Strategies of Curriculum Transaction	81
3. Education of the Trainable Mentally Challenged	81
Prevention of Mental Retardation	83
Review Questions	84
5. Giftedness	**85**
Learning Objectives	85
Who is a Gifted Child?	86
Causes of Giftedness	87
The Concept of Mental Age and IQ	88
Charateristics of Gifted Children	89
Educational Practices	94
Problems of Gifted Children	100
Review Questions	101

6. Learning Disabilities **103**
Symptoms of Learning Difficulties 106
Causes of Learning Disabilities 110
Identification of Learning Disabled Children 112
Types of Learning Disabilities 114
Educational Provisions for the Learning Disabled 116
Review Questions 117

7. Autism **118**
Objectives of the Lesson 119
Causes 120
Educational Procedures 121
Methodology 121
Review Questions 122

8. The Creative Child **123**
Defining Creativity 123
Characteristics of Creative Person 124
Identification of Creative Potential 125
Creativity Tests 125
Problems of Creativity 127
Educating the Creative Children 128
Review Questions 131

9. Educational Backwardness **132**
Barton Hall (1947) 133
Schonell (1948) 133
Burt (1950) 133
Causes of Backwardness 134
Identification of Backwardness 136
Characteristics of Backward Children 139
Education of the Backward Children 139
Review Questions 142

10. Behavioural Disorders and Emotional Disturbances **143**
Learning Objectives 144
Meaning and Definition 144
Characteristics of BD/ED 145

Causes of BD/ED 147
Rehabilitation and Care 150
Review Questions 151

11. Rehabilitation Services 152
Rehabilitation 152
Rehabilitation of the Planning and Execution 152
Rights of Disabled 153
Difficulties in Identifying the Disabled 154
NGOs and Rehabilitation 155
Review Questions 156

References 157

Index 158

1

Children with Special Needs

Introduction

India was one of the few countries in South Asia which signed in the Proclamation on the Full Participation and Equality of People with Disabilities in the Asian and Pacific Region when the Asian and Pacific Decade of Disabled Persons was initiated, in 1993-2002. It lays emphasis on improving the living conditions of people with disabilities at the initial stage itself so that they will not get aggravated and to some extent they could be minimized at the initial stage itself.

As per the 2001 Census there are 21,906,769 persons in India who have visual, communication, loco motor disabilities and mental retardation. This statistics includes 12,605,635 male and 9,301,134 female. The Government suggested that the teacher-pupil ratio should be 1:8 for mentally challenged and 1:2 for multiple disabled.

Persons with disabilities are those who are born with a disability, who acquire due to micro nutrients deficiencies, become disabled in between due to accidents or trauma or some events in their life. Some may have single disability and some may have multiple disabilities. Besides their suffering from these disabilities they have other disadvantages and obstacles also. They face social, economic, cultural and physical barriers in the community. These severely affect their active participation in the life of their communities on equal terms like their normal partners.

All these indicate that efforts are to be taken to bring these people with disabilities on par with other children, who are without disabilities by providing health care services, education, vocational training and rehabilitation. This will enable them to develop self-confidence, self-esteem and independence to stand on their own legs without depending on others and be a burden to their families, the society and the nation.

Special efforts have been taken by Government departments and Non-Governmental Agencies to provide health care services, education, vocational training and rehabilitation arrangements in India. Lot of fund has been allotted for these programmes. Initiatives have been taken to create awareness among the people that disability is not due to any sin committed either by parents or fore parents of which they have to be ashamed.

Children with Special Needs—Definitions and Classification

It is not an easy task to define an exceptional child or a child with special needs, or a child with disabilities though many have attempted. The problem becomes more difficult when an exceptional child or a child with special needs is studied through various disciplines like Psychology, Sociology, Physiology, Medicine and Education. And each discipline studies the exceptional child from different perspective and different angles.

In the words of Samuel A. Kulu, "An exceptional child is that child who deviates from the average or normal child in Mental, Physical, or Social characteristics to such an extent that he/she requires a modification of school practices or special educational services in order to develop to his/her maximum capacity." A child with special needs requires not only education; it needs to learn as to how he/she has to adjust to live in this world. This definition says that an educationally exceptional child is one who requires a modification in the education programme to meet his/her specific needs. The usual classroom activities in a special school, where there is less opportunity for interaction with normal children cannot help him/her much. They should be brought into normal classroom situations where there will be more opportunities to move with other children without disability. This inclusive education will improve the self-confidence and self-esteem of children with disabilities.

There should be a paradigm shift from disability viewed as a medical or psychological problem to disability groups calling for access to equal opportunity in the society. They do not require our sympathy, they are to be treated and given equal opportunities in life. We have to consider their abilities not disabilities. Each disability need is to be properly diagnosed and treated differently and then brought to the main stream. Parents care takers and the teachers have equal responsibility in this great task. Then the whole community should come forward to rehabilitate the children with special needs. It is through the collective efforts and strength of any nation as a whole, with the partnership of government, social organizations and the community alone this problem be tackled and reduced. People with disabilities are a valuable human resource which is often left untapped. This reservoir of human capabilities should be viewed from the perspective of employability, if we help them achieve any measure of self-reliance.

Children with special needs or disability or the exceptional children are broadly classified as Mentally Challenged, Physically Challenged and Socially and Emotionally Challenged or Children with Behavioural Problems. Each category has been further classified according to the disabilities as shown here under:

Differently Abled Children

Mentally challenged	Physically challenged	Socially and Emotionally Challenged
1. Gifted	1. Orthopaedically handicapped	1. Delinquents
2. Backward	2. Visually impaired	2. Problem Children
3. Retarded	3. Hearing impaired	
	4. Speech impaired	

Classification of Children with Special Needs or Differently Abled

Attempt has been made in this book and specifically in the following chapter to help the readers understand who is a special or differently abled child and the need to understand their requirement and their responsibilities in solving the problems of the children with disabilities. And this will help them to have positive thinking about themselves and try to contribute to the society in spite of their disabilities.

Efforts taken to Solve/Combat the Problems of Children with Special Needs

All the children who are differently abled require special attention and efforts are being taken to bring them back to normalcy or to help them stand on their own legs without depending on others. They need comprehensive spectrum of care and services. The families of these children also need some counselling and services so that they also become partners in reducing/solving/combating the problems of children with special needs. Services to these children begin with early screening and diagnosing the problems and the services needed, which include Medical, Daycare, Education and Rehabilitation. Service providers should periodically assess the adequacy, correctness, and the delivery mode to the recipients. This will help the service institutions to modify or change the system of services provided to suit and be of maximum benefits to the recipients of the services. Some may need prolonged medical aids as out patients and some may need hospitalization. These requirements are to be periodically assessed.

Some children need special education in a special school for a longer period to learn basic skills. Whereas some may be very quick and fast in learning the basic skills such as reading, writing and arithmetic needed for formal education and become ready to be admitted in the normal school for inclusive education. Even in the normal school few children with special needs may need special resource room and more special assistance and some may easily adjust to the strategies followed for normal children.

Some children may be ready to learn a skill required for an occupation without much difficultly. Whereas a few may require prolonged efforts to be ready for any occupation and a few may not be able to pick up any vocational skill needed for their rehabilitation. Depending on the degree and type of disability we need to follow an integrated approach to provide service system to the children with special needs.

It is a challenging task to take care of the children with special needs, at home by the parents, the doctors in the hospital, teachers in the school and the public in the society. No one can be successful without the support of all the agencies that are involved in the service-providing task. An integrated approach, with the support of the Government alone could provide a wholesome service delivery system, to combat or to solve the problems of children with special needs.

Education and Care of Children with Special Needs

It may be a shock to the parents when a child is born with a disability. But they should soon accept the fact that their child needs all their love, care and help. This enables the child born with disability feel that his/her family has accepted to be a member of the family and thus develop self-confidence to develop other abilities. If such children are hidden and felt ashamed of, then others will also ignore him/her. The growth of the other traits will also be retarded and social participation will also be affected, leading to a negative feeling.

Special education programme is gaining importance today. Parents and the public have started realising their responsibility of caring, educating and rehabilitating the children who need special attention and care. The state also takes equal responsibility in this great endeavour. On reading this module the reader should have achieved the following objectives:

Learning Objectives

- Understand the meaning of special education.
- Realize the importance of special education.

- Identify the reasons for providing special education.
- Classify different types of special education programme.
- Analyze the relative importance of each type.
- Describe the merit and difficulties faced in each type.
- List the strategies and techniques to be followed in special education.
- Specify the role of parents, care takers and teachers in the rehabilitation of disabled.
- Have a vision of special education in future.

Purpose of Special Education

The purpose of Special Education is to advance and develop the abilities of children with special needs such as Physical, Emotional, Mental and Social and enable their integration into general education system, if possible society and the work force. It also includes providing physiotherapy, speech therapy and occupational therapy according to the child's needs.

Individual with Disabilities Education Act (IDEA) defines special education as specially designed instruction to meet the unique needs of a student with a disability.

Whether special education is to be given to the children with disabilities, could be given in a regular classroom, a special education class room with in a regular school or a separate special education school is to be decided on the basis of the degree of disability of the child, assessed by expert group. Children who are admitted in exclusive special school get special treatment, care, therapy and services needed for the particular disability. Where as disabled children admitted within a general educational system may not get all these special services except services like providing Braille equipment for the visually impaired, hearing aids to the children with hearing impairment and remedial instruction to children with learning disability etc.

It becomes the responsibility of the parents, psychologists who diagnoses and the educator to decide which type of education would be suitable to their children, on the basis of the degree of disability. If the disability is mild or moderate, initially special education could be given in special schools and then these children can be brought to the main stream in the regular school and provided with integrated schooling. Basic skills needed for the disabled can be taught in the special schools. According to the Persons with Disability Act, 1995 disabled children are to be covered either under "special school" or integrated to mainstream school. Though there are controversial opinion about both it is the duty/responsibility of the parents and the teachers to decide which would be better for their children with disability.

The Future of Special Education

In spite of the efforts by the Government and non-Governmental Agencies to care, educate and rehabilitate persons with disabilities they are awaiting the opportunities and are excluded and remain out of school. But still a collative effort is needed to take care of medical requirement and educational requirement of all with disabilities. All must be educated in the classroom settings. In future they should say that there are no people who are "non-educable"; "All children can learn till they are capable at least to take care of themselves".

Special education helps the children with disabilities to achieve their full potentials. Special education provides the opportunities to learn, read, write and compute. These skills are provided according to their capabilities and appropriate for their disabilities. These children with disabilities need, not only the skill of reading, writing and arithmetic; they should also develop social skills, communication skills and the ability to adjust with the community. With all these opportunities they can be prepared for a job or vocation and become economically independent in future.

With the right education, the disabled can cope with high level and responsible occupations on equal terms with abled persons. It is the key to the development, either personal, social, economic, political or even spiritual. Educations plays an important role in making children aware of their own potentials, capabilities and aspirations and perform accordingly.

The purpose of special Education is to advance and develop the abilities of children with special needs so that they could move to integrated schooling, into the society and workforce with ease and they need not be a burden to society. The community should come forward to use the potentials of these children with special needs, who have special talents.

Special education first and then the integrated programme should be made available in the communities closer to their homes. Special education with physiotherapy, speech therapy and occupational therapy will enable the children with special needs to return to the mainstream of the society.

Inclusive Education

In the early years medical model of care was followed than the educational approach. So any disability was considered as an illness and treated in institutions, by taking them away from the main stream of the society. Where as educational approach emphasizes on bringing into the main stream of the society by integrating them in the normal schools. It is necessary for the disabled to experience an independent and normalized life. Education in an open and free atmosphere will promote the growth of the disabled in an unrestricted way. Inclusive education with normal children will make friends and belongingness to a group. It will also enable the normal children to accept the disabled as equal members of the society, rather than objects of ridicule or pity.

Inclusion of children with disabilities into the General Education System would be the best option to satisfy the requirements of these children and to make use of their talents with out much expenditure. Hence, priority should be given to the integration of special children in the general stream of education. This inclusive education helps the children with disabilities to develop self-confidence and acquire normal behavioural skills needed for leading a normal life with less dependency or live independently.

At the same time we should also consider whether it is proper to put these children with special needs along with normal children without proper preparation. A child with hearing impairment needs the help of an audio-graphic or a communication specialist and a proper acoustic condition for learning; Braille equipment is needed for a child with visual impairment, a child with learning disabilities needs remedial instruction. Is it possible to provide all these facilities in every school is a big question mark? If these children are admitted into the inclusive school without considering the above issues it will become a problem not only to the children with disabilities, but also to the school authorities to manage the situations.

Hence, it is suggested that till they complete the primary schooling or upto 5th standard, children with needs be admitted into special schools meant for specific disability, acquire needed skills and then get admitted into inclusive school. Parents should also get acquainted with specific skills needed for their children so that they can also support their children in normal school system. This satisfies the rights of children with special needs, to learn together with children of their own age, to take part in the culture of children of their own age group and social structure of their own communities.

Effective Special Education Programme

Disabled children develop physical, psychological and social insecurity and lose self-confidence and generate feeling of hatred and hostility towards normal children. When they are isolated there will be gulf between the disabled and others causing poor communication skills and mobility. All these may make the disabled sensitive, aggressive and slowly withdraw from others, become lonely.

Irrespective of kind, category and degree of disability education should be provided to all in a conducive and appropriate atmosphere. We have to follow "zero rejection" policy by adopting same form of education for all the children with special needs. The approaches may be Home based education, Non-formal, Informal, Open, Distance learning, Alternative schooling, Community based rehabilitations and vocational education.

Components of the Special Education Programme

1. Early detection and identification: While taking the household survey itself, if a strategy is adopted to identify the children with special needs they can have an early intervention programme at home itself and followed at daycare and early childhood education centres.

2. Functional and formal assessment: Formal assessment by experts and their suggestion for appropriate care for the child with special needs will help them to be placed appropriately in the community.

3. Placement services: Enroll every child to have education either in a special school or in an inclusive school after providing basic skills needed for the specific disability.

4. Teaching Learning Materials: Provide teaching aids, instructional materials and appliances required for learning and teaching these children.

5. Provision of Support Services: Support services like physical access, resource rooms, special equipments, and materials for teaching and learning, remedial teaching, special techniques of teaching and appropriate curriculum are to be made available in the school for special education or in the inclusive school.

6. Teacher education: Teachers have to play an important role in educating children with special needs. It is not enough they possess teaching skills; they should have an aptitude for teaching children with special needs. They are to be sensitized and given special training in the teacher education programme.

7. Individualized instruction: Children with special needs require individual attention and treatment. This could be done only after identifying the special needs of each child in consultation with experts and parents.

8. Parental training and community mobilization: Parents of children with disabilities try to disown them some time, as they think that it is a sin to have such children. They must be counselled first to accept their children and then to be trained to look after them. Every child with disability is to be taken care of according to the disability. Community should also be mobilized and motivated to take care of special children as its responsibility.

9. Strengthening special schools: Besides the resource teachers in the normal schools, the special schools should also be strengthened with the support of the Governmental and Non-Governmental Organizations (NGOs).

10. Disabled friendly atmosphere: Architectural barriers in the schools and colleges should be removed and provide disabled friendly facilities to their easy movement.

All the above approaches and strategies discussed will be fruitful and functional only when there is participatory and integrated approach in the care, education and rehabilitation of children with special needs. It should become everybody's responsibility.

Review Questions

Who is a special child or differently abled?

Classify the children with special needs.

Why should we give special education to differently abled?

How will you identify children with special needs?

Describe the problems faced by differently abled children.

Analyze the efforts taken to combat the problems of differently abled.

How will you convince the public that it is their responsibility to take care of the disabled?

As an individual interested in the welfare of the disabled suggest steps to be taken to solve the problems of the disabled children.

2

Physical and Health Impairment

The problems of physical and health impairment have been duly recognized these days. Orthopaedically/physically handicapped are those who suffer from a defect that is accompanied by one or another type of deformity that inhibits the normal exercise of his/her muscles, joints or bones. Health impairment refers to condition in which the body's physical well-being is affected, requiring some form of medical attention. This package gives you more information on:

— The types of orthopaedically/physically impaired,
— Causes of physical impairment,
— Methods of identification, and
— Educational provisions for physically impaired children.

Learning Objectives

On completion of this package, readers will be able to:

1. Define orthopaedically handicapped/physically impaired
2. List the types of orthopaedically handicapped/physically impaired
3. Enumerate the causes of orthopaedic handicaps/physically impairment
4. Identify orthopaedically handicapped children
5. Describe the educational provision for orthopaedically/physially handicapped
6. Identify and arrange appropriate rehabilitation programme for them.

Definition

Who are these orthopaedically handicapped or physically impaired or crippled children? Psychologists disagree on any single definition of the term given here: 'A child whose arms or either legs or all four limbs are damaged may be called crippled'. The loss of one arm/one leg will not classify a person as totally crippled. The loss refers to the inability to use and not necessarily their physical absence. A child with physical difficulties has a problem with structure and functioning of the body.

Individual with Disabilities Education Act (IDEA): Defines the orthopaedic impairment as follows:

The term 'includes' impairment caused by congenital anomaly (e.g. clubfoot), impairment caused by diseases like Poliomyelitis, bone tuberculosis etc., and impairment from other causes, such as Cerebral Palsy, amputations, fractures etc. Sometime it appears in combination with other disabilities.

Types of Orthopaedic/Physical Disabilities

Following are some of the physical and special health problems of children, who need special care and rehabilitation programmes at home, school and society. Their major requirement is mobility training. Special wheel chairs motorized, computerized and even race wheel chairs are available for easy independent mobility. They may also select artificial limbs or electrical walking machines. A recent invention of robotics also helps those who have lost their arms. Robotic arms can manipulate the objects.

Cerebral Palsy

Cerebral Palsy has been defined as 'a motor disability caused by a brain dysfunction'. There are different types of Cerebral Palsies.

1. Spastic Paralysis: It is caused by damaged brain. It is paralysis of one (or) more limbs. For example:

(a) *Hemiplegia*: One side of body is affected.
(b) *Priplegia*: Three limbs affected (2 legs, 1 arm).

(c) *Monoplegia*: One limb is affected.
(d) *Paraplegia*: Both legs affected.
(e) *Quadriplegia*: All four limbs affected.
(f) *Biplegia*: Both upper extremities affected.

2. *Erb's Palsy*: This type of palsy occurs when one shoulder is caught under pelvic rim during pregnancy and the child loses sensation of arms.

3. *Athetosis*: This condition is caused by a lesion in the extra pyramidal system located in the forebrain or middle brain, and is characterized by involuntary motion by the parts of the body.

4. *Ataxia*: A lesion in the cerebellum, which controls balance and muscle coordination, causes Ataxia. Unsteady movements, walking with a high step, falling easily, lack of balance, jerky movements—all these are behavioural disorders of this child. Chronic health conditions like allergies, asthma, cancer, diabetics, HN substance and kidney disease.

5. *Termor and Rigidity*: This is caused due to injury in extra pyramidal system. The body of the infant shows involuntary vibratory movements.

6. *Sickle cell Anemia*: It is a genetic disorder which is caused by distortion and malfunction of the red blood cells reducing the supply of oxygen resulting in severe pain.

Causes and Prevention of Orthopaedical Handicap or Physical and Health Disabilities

The causative factors of all types of handicaps are many and are listed here:

***1. Pre-natal causes*:** Genetic and inherited condition during pregnancy affects the nervous system, resulting in congenital anomaly of spinal muscular atrophy.

(a) *Prenatal anoxia*: Caused by premature separation of placenta.

(*b*) *Severe anemia*: If during pregnancy, the mother suffers from anemia, the child also suffers from orthopaedic handicap or is born with physical impairments.
(*c*) *Abortion*: An aborted child suffers Cerebral Palsy.
(*d*) *RH factor*: Is also responsible for physical impairments.

2. Post-natal Conditions: Cerebral Palsy is caused by:

(*a*) diseases like—meningitis, influenza, typhoid etc.
(*b*) head injury from accidents
(*c*) poisoning
(*d*) strangulation

3. Congenital Amputations: Most childhood amputations are the result of trauma or congenial anomaly. Artificial replacement is aimed at to maintain the functioning of the limb. Some examples are:

(*a*) *Torticollis*: caused by contraction of the neck muscles drawing the head to the side with chin pointing in the opposite direction.
(*b*) *Arthrograposis*: caused due to incomplete muscle development in early embryonic period. Others are postural foot conditions, juvenile rheumatoid arthritis, dislocated hips etc.

4. Postural Defects: Postural defects may develop in children due to malnutrition, carelessness of parents, muscular weakness etc. (e.g. unequal length of the legs).

In general, various causes can be classified broadly under three heads as:

(*a*) Hereditary causes
(*b*) Congenital causes
(*c*) Acquired causes (which include all birth injuries, accidents, nutrition deficiency, defective bones and joints, viral infections etc.).

Identification of Orthopaedically Handicapped/Physically Impaired

Identification of orthopaedically handicapped children is very easy when compared with other disabilities like partial sightedness and hearing impairment etc. For these children, identification can be made with the help of the following checklist on behavioural manifestations.

1. Physically impaired children have poor motor control and co-ordination.
2. They walk awkwardly or with a limp.
3. These children show signs of pain during physical exercise.
4. They fall frequently.
5. Show symptoms of poor health condition.

Educational Provisions

Before deciding the educational provisions for crippled/physically impaired children, and children with health problems we must acknowledge that they are similar in all respects to normal children. In educating them we should keep in mind the following provisions:

1. Equality of Educational Opportunity

Constitution of India has provided equality of educational opportunity for all children without discrimination of caste, colour, creed and status. Schools must be provided with the facilities to meet the physical needs of these children. Transportation facility must be provided so that they can have easy mobility and attend the school.

2. Educational Programmes must Recognize the Handicaps and Health Condition

The child's physical handicap and health condition should be taken into consideration while planning for education. Each child should

Help to Move and Co-ordinate

On the Wheels

We Too Want to Contest

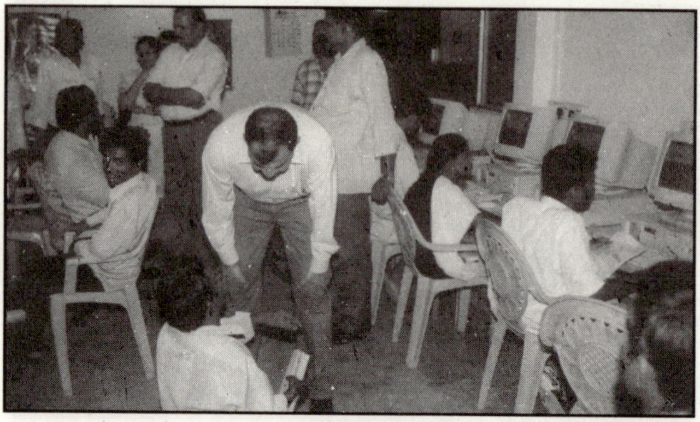

Computer Literacy

Learning a Vocation-Binding

Learning a Vocation-Tailoring

Promoting a Different Skill

I too can Help

be helped to realize the problem he/she will façe in entering occupation where physical conditions may interfere.

3. Develop Initiative and Self-reliance

The crippled children should not be over-protected and dependent. They should be taught to do things for themselves and to assume initiation in the development and completion of school projects. The parents must be encouraged to accept this and develop positive attitude towards the child with the disability.

4. Minimum Retention

Retain the children at home as long as parental care is required and then send them to school. The crippled/physically impaired child should be retained in school as long as he needs its help and is able to get along with others and acquires the basic skills.

5. Home Instruction

Instruction at home can be provided to those children who are unable to move out of their home. Such children may include physically impaired/crippled, cardiac, chronic health problems, epileptic and psycho-neurotics. A specially trained teacher for educating homebound children is deputed for instruction at home. In addition the home-to-school phone and tele-teaching can be made available to motivate children and give them opportunity to participate in a broader environment. Home instruction needs active participation of parents to plan education of such children. The teacher should be adaptable to the needs of the individual child and must have broad interests and willingness to extend his help beyond the conventional 'routine duty' and the ability to plan and work independently.

6. School in the Hospital

This is the method of providing school facilities in a hospital. Teaching in hospital will be conducted either at the child's bed side or in separate place. The teachers in such schools are *bona fide* members of hospital team and participate in case conferences. The teacher modifies his programme of instruction according to the needs of the child.

7. Special Schools and Classes

To bridge the gap between home or care in a hospital and instruction and attendance in a regular classroom, special classes and special schools have been established for children with physical disabilities. Special classes for physically disabled children are organized to meet their special needs in a disabled friendly environment. Classes are held on the ground floor of the building, so that problem of mobility is minimized. Special equipment is provided for disabled children according to the type of disability. Efforts are taken to develop the potentialities of disabled children to the maximum. But now separate schools are also recommended for those children who are severely and profoundly handicapped and suffer from health problems where holding separate classes is absolutely necessary. This will enable them to acquire essential skills first then join the main stream.

8. Education in General Classroom with the Support of Special Teacher

The disabled children are instructed with non-handicapped children in general classroom. If the regular teacher has any instructional problem, he/she seeks the guidance of the special teacher on the problem.

9. Education in General Classroom with Provision for Special Instruction

Here, the disabled children study with normal children but also attend part time special instruction through a special teacher who caters to the individual needs.

Review Questions

1. Define Orthopaedically handicapped/Physically Impaired. How will you identify them?
2. As a Primary-school teacher suggest the specific characteristics of orthopaedically handicapped found in the classrooms and the suitable educational provisions for those children.
3. How will you classify types of physical disabilities?
4. Analyze the causes of physical disabilities.
5. Describe the characteristics of orthopaedically/physically impaired.
6. What types of rehabilitation should be provided to physically disabled?
7. How will you educate the children with physical and health impairment?

3

Sensory Disabilities

Sensory disability consists of objectively defined impairment of structure and functions of sensory organs. Such eyes, ears and speech organs. There is no much difference between these children and the normal ones in their psychological make-up. They have their own exceptionalities and influences in society. These children are educationally handicapped and cannot avail of education through normal system. They need special education and help. In this package let us discuss about children who are visually impaired or blind have speech disorder, the deaf and dumb or hearing impairment.

— The types of sensory disabilities,
— Causes of sensory disabilities, and
— The educational provisions.

Learning Objectives

On completion of reading this package, reader will be able to:

1. Define
(a) visually impaired
(b) aurally impaired
(c) speech impairment

2. Identify
(a) visually impaired
(b) aurally impaired
(c) speech impaired

3. ***Explain the causes of***
   (a) visual
   (b) aural, and
   (c) speech impairment
4. ***Analyze the problems of children with***
   (a) visual impairment
   (b) aural impairment, and
   (c) speech impairment
5. ***Describe the educational provisions of children with***
   (a) visual
   (b) aural
   (c) speech impairment
6. ***List the types of***
   (a) visual impairment
   (b) aural, and
   (c) speech
7. Understand the role of parents; care takers, peer group and the teachers in taking care of children with sensory disabilities—visual, aural and speech.

I. VISUALLY IMPAIRED OR BLIND

Ramesh six years old boy when admitted in the first standard was asked to interpret the pictures and tell stories with the assistance of the pictures. He was looking down to see the picture or keeping it very close to his eyes. The teacher asked the parents to take him to an ophthalmologist. When Ramesh was screened it was found that his vision was very low, reported as 20/120. As he was very young, immediate attention and functional vision examination helped him to see better. He is able to adjust with the normally sighted children in the school. Inclusive education, with the glass is advantageous to him now.

Whereas Vimala was born blind. The parents were guiding the girl patiently and taught her some social and personal skills needed for her to do her own personal work and move around at home. When she was six years old they wanted her to get formal education and took her to a special school for visually impaired.

After undergoing all the tests, including emotional stability test, she was admitted in the school. It was an ungraded schooling system which they followed in the school so that the children could learn according to their own pace without much pressure. She was given training in personal life skills, including the mobility training. Reading, writing and mathematical skills with the assistance of Braille. The child now learns through touch the academic programme using Braille.

There are many more such cases, we find in our school. As parents, care takers and teachers it is our responsibility to take care of children. When they grow up they need some vocation to take care of themselves.

Vision plays an important role in development of concepts; the understanding of spatial and using printed materials. These areas are significantly affected when the vision is affected.

Blindness is regarded as the most severe and traumatic physical handicap. Since more impressions are conveyed to the brain through the eyes, the visual anomalies may influence the life of the individual in physical, mental social, vocational and educational aspects. Visual handicap is the inability to see within normal limits.

Who is Visually Impaired or Blind?

IDEA defines visual disability and blinders as impairment in vision that even with correction adversely affects a child's educational performance. Visual efficiency is influenced by two factors: activity and peripheral vision. Visual activity describes how well a person can see at various distances. The width of a person's field of vision or the ability to perceive objects. Outside the direct line of vision is called peripheral vision.

Classification

Children with visual impairment can be classified into three: low vision, functionally blind and totally blind, on the basis of their ability to use their vision.

People with low vision can read enlarged print with optical aids such as magnifying glasses. There people may not be legally considered blind as they could read with the help of magnifying lenses. They are also called partially sighted. This interferes with learning and daily functioning also.

Functionally blind people use Braille, a specially developed method, for reading and writing. For mobility and other activities they may use the limited vision they have, along with tactile sensation and auditory ability.

Totally blind cannot have any stimuli through vision, as they do not receive any meaningful image through visual sense. They completely depend on tactual and auditory senses for their adjustment with the environment.

Blindness can also be educationally classified as:

***1. Blind*:** All individuals who need special arrangement for their instruction.

***2. Partially Blind*:** Those children who have problem in their vision can be taught with normal children with special arrangement.

***3. Colour Blind*:** Colour blindness is a disease in which individual does not see colours.

Identification of Visually Impaired

The identification of visual impairment is related to some behavioural symptoms, and communicated by them observed when uses eyes for reading for long.

1. Complains of headache
2. Covers one eye and thrusts the head forward
3. Rubs eye excessively
4. Holds objects including books close to her/his eyes
5. Blinks eye frequently
6. Asks other children to read aloud when taking notes from the blackboard
7. The pupils of the eye dilate often
8. Smaller eye-lids/Red-rimmed eyes

9. Seems very sensitive to light
10. Watering of eyes
11. Takes false steps while walking
12. Squint eyes
13. Becomes inattentive during reading sessions
14. Don't move around spontaneously through environment.

Total blindness can easily be recognized. But a detailed examination is needed to recognize partially blind children. Snelleu chart is used to measure the vision activity, by reading the chart from 20 feet, the alphabets 20/20 is considered typical.

Causes of Visual Impairment

Structures within the eye and its visual pathway play important roles in seeing involve transmission of light energy through the eyes and conversion of this to electrical energy. This is the transmission of electrical impulses to the brain for interpretation. When there is impairment and malfunctioning in these processes it leads to blindness or visual impairment.

The main causes of blindness are congenital (present at birth) or acquired. In addition, lack of proper medical treatment, infection and diseases etc. also cause visual handicaps. Dust, heat, smoke and deficiency diseases lead to partial blindness, night blindness, colour blindness etc.

(i) ***Infectious Diseases***: Mostly 60 to 70 per cent of children become blind due to infectious diseases. Blood disorders can also cause blindness.

(ii) ***Accident or Injury***: Lack of safety and guidance, fight or accident cause blindness, among children.

(iii) ***Hereditary***: Sometimes, blindness is inherited and congenital. However, the frequency of such occurrences is very significant.

(iv) ***Common Diseases***: Blindness also occurs due to various physical diseases, such as diabetes, vitamin deficiency etc.

(v) ***Effect of Poisons***: Effect of poison is also one of the factors that account for blindness.

(vi) Other causes are Albinism, cataract, Glaucoma, muscular degeneration, myopia, Optic move atrophy, Retinities pigmentosa, and Retinopathy of prematurity.

Characteristics and Problems of Visually Impaired

The visually impaired children confront with many problems in their life. They rule their eyes excessively, shuts or covers one eye, shows difficulty in reading, blinks often, holds book close to eyes, unable to see distant things clearly, squints, eyes are crossed, red rimmed, swollen eyelids, inflamed or water eyes, eyes itch, burn or feel scratchy, cannot see well, dizziness, headache or nausea and blurred or double vision are some of the characteristics of children with visual impairment.

(i) ***Poor Intelligence*:** Research analyses reveal that visually impaired children have a poor I.Q. Since they have impairments in the exploration of their environments, they have impairments also in concept formation resulting in poor performance in intelligence tests. Some intelligence tests measure degrees of information, knowledge or experience the individual possess. But for blind children, this pattern of scoring is reduced to very low level.

(ii) ***Academic Retardation*:** Visually impaired children have poor academic achievement even if they use large types of Brailles. They have slower reading rate, lack concreteness in instructional procedures. They are noted to be retarded at least by one or two years than the normal children, of their age.

(iii) ***Slower Speech Development*:** Totally blind children cannot learn the art of speech by imitation, as they cannot see or observe the lip movements. They can learn through what they hear, touch and observe. Progress in speech development is not significant in comparison with normal children.

(iv) ***Personality Disorder*:** For blind children, life experiences go in their own ways which are totally different from

Visually Impaired

Early Intervention

Learning Maths

In the Class

Braile Learning

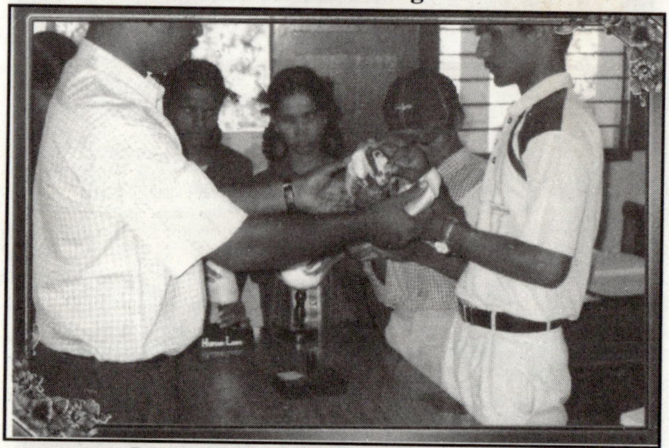

Learning Science—Touch Method

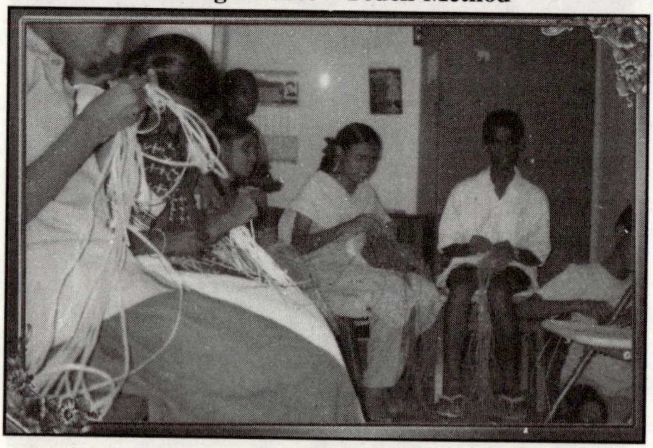

Vocational Training

Learning Music

Sports Activities

normal children. These differences affect their personality as a whole. Due to this she/he experiences nervous strain, feeling of insecurity and frustration.

(v) ***Problems in Social Adjustment:*** Normally these children are looked down or ridiculed by normal children every now and then. Because of this they feel inferiority, which ultimately leads to maladjustment.

Educational Provisions

1. Partiality Sighted

(a) Medical Care: If the teacher discovers a partially blind child, he/she may bring the case to the notice of the primary health centre or hospital for an eye check-up. His/her parents must be informed immediately, and be aware of their child's difficulty in seeing, for further treatment.

(b) Special Arrangements: The District Educational authority should arrange special classes for these children. The school must be centrally located and good transport facilities must be available. Hostel and boarding facilities must be made available for rural children.

Visually impaired children have difficulty in acquiring many life skills, including social skills. Orientation and mobility are important areas that need special attention so that they could adjust to their environment and learn how to move around safely. This includes development of body image, concrete environmental concepts, directional concepts, orientation skills, independent travel in various situations and public interaction skills.

(c) Introducing Co-curricular Activities: The extra and co-curricular activities, if introduced in the schools will help the partially blind child overcome his/her inferiority by participating in any activities of his/her interest and choice. Skills required to participate in life skill activities must be taught. Child should develop communication skills such as listening, hand writing, use of sensory motor skills, daily life skills such as personal hygiene, eating, dressing, preparation of food, identification of money, use of telephone, shopping, concept of time, date etc.

(d) Minimum Visual Tasks: Partially sighted must be provided with minimum visual tasks. Delicate mathematical constructions, laboratory work and meticulous observations are to be strictly prohibited for these children.

(e) Attitude of Parents and Teachers: Parents, teachers and friends must be sympathetic towards these children. They must show much affection and adhesiveness. They must keep in mind that these children should not feel inferior in anyway.

(f) Classroom Arrangement:

(i) The teacher must see that in the class, these children are seated in front benches and assign some sighted children to sit next, so that they could help with mobility in emergency.

(ii) The letters written on board should be legible and unambiguous.

(iii) The teacher has to speak as he/she writes on the board.

(iv) Books with bold letters should be kept in the library and for reading, along with Braille books.

(a) Residential School: Residential schools are highly beneficial for blind children. These schools assist the children through the use of special methods and aids.

(b) Special Equipment: For Blind, the medium of education should be different, since these children require education through touch and hearing Braille method which used a coded system of the dots enclosed on papers should be used special attention should be given to practice on a regular typewriter. Educational trips, teaching with models, working with clay and plastics give pleasure to these children.

(c) Physical Education: Though blind children are very much restricted for physical activities special attention could be paid to teach swimming, rowing, and handicrafts household arts and squall skills.

(d) Vocational Programme: Sheltered workshops for the blind are really conducive. The vocational emphasis on these workshops on preparation of things like brooms, rugs and brushes.. Vocational skills like knitting, singing, using musical instruments etc. could be taught so that on completion of their education they could take up some vocation and stand on their own.

Training provided in development of various skills will also help the individual to earn their lively hood.

Prevention

Proper medical care and nutrition during prenatal period, during delivery and during early childhood could reduce the assurance of the visual impairment. A environment and safety educators can prevent accident causing visual impairment. Similarly early diagnosis will prevent aggravation of the impairment. Proper training in orientation and mobility Independence will increase their self-confidence and reduce accidents. Orientation is the mental map people have about their surroundings and the mobility is the ability to travel safely and efficiently from one place to another.

II. SPEECH DISORDERS

Delipan is a student of 5th standard. Whenever he speaks he repeats certain sounds and sometimes takes time to utter words. This makes others laugh at him. Delipan is upset when his friends laugh at him. Parents also noticed this defective speech pattern of their son. But they found that the boy has been imitating his father who stammers and shutters. He was doing it unconsciously; but he inherited this character from his father, which continues. After Delipan's admission into the school, when it was noticed that the boy was made fun of, by his peer group, they consulted a doctor. Then they found on interviewing the parents that Delipan was following his father's speech pattern. As it is an acquired disorder the speech the rapist said that it could be corrected by providing speech therapy.

Kamala, at the age of four was referred to a doctor, as she was not able to produce the sounds properly and was showing withdrawal behaviour. On identifying that this disorder was due to left lip and left palate the child had. He suggested that it could be corrected through a small surgery. After the surgery Kamala was referred to a speech pathologist who have her a constant speech therapy and now Kamala tries to speak like other children in her class.

These are the two cases of speech impairment one is acquired, the other is organic genetic.

Speech is the expression of language in sound form. It includes producing, the speech sounds, voicing the speech pitch and loudness. Speech sounds are produced when air passes through the vocal tract, i.e. larynx, pharynx, mouth and nose. Due to various positions of lips, tongue and jaw the sound is formed. During first eight years chi'dren learn to produce all the consonants, vowels and diphthongs. These sounds, which result in speech, may vary depending on pitch (rate of vibration of vocal folds); and intensity (loudness—pressure coming from lungs). Resonance (how the tone which comes from vocal fold is modified by the cavities of throat, mouth and nose); and the quality of the voice is related to all the above three.

Fluency in speech is the result of easy, smooth and effortless flow of speech. When disturbances occur in these it leads to speech disorder or impairment. Nearly 8 per cent of the population has some form of communication disorder.

"Speech and language disorders are observed disturbances in the normal speech, language or learning process" (Palmer Syantis, 1990).

This interferes with communication and makes both the speaker and the listener uncomfortable. This situation need not be due to loss of hearing or deafness.

According to IDEA, "speech or language impairment means a communication disorder such as stuttering, impaired articulation, a language impairment or a voice impairment that adversely affect a child's educational performance".

These are called speech disorders. It is due to problems in sending or debarring messages. Language disorder indicates the problem in receiving, understanding and formulating messages. Speech disorder indicates that there is an impairments as the articulation of speech sounds, fluency and or voice" (American speech—Language—Learning Association, 1993).

Definitions

Jon Eielson defines speech defect as:

'Any child who speaks so that attention is distracted from what is being said to the manner of its production may be considered to have speech defect.'

According to Van Riper 'Speech is said to be abnormal when it deviates so far from the speech of other people, that it calls attention to itself, interferes with communication or causes discomfort or distress to the speaker or listener."

Therefore, it is pertinent that a child's speech is defective when the amount of distraction is sufficient to make it difficult for him to communicate readily with a normal listener.

Causes of Speech Impairment

The following may be the possible causes of speech impairment, which may be of organic or acquired disorders. Organic disorders may originate from nervous system, the muscular system or the formation of the mouth, nose and other organs needed for speech. These disorders may be due to heredity, genetic, malformation, prenatal injury, and infectious and muscular diseases. Acquired disorders may occur due to accident or some events in the life of an individual that affect negatively.

(1) *Loss of hearing*: If a child has impaired hearing he/she cannot listen what others speak in the environment. There is every possibility that he/she may develop speech handicap.
(2) *Long Illness*: Prolonged illness may lead to speech impairment.
(3) *Emotional disturbance*: If a child is emotionally disturbed, her/his speech may be affected. For example, sudden loss of a parent.
(4) *Deformation of ear*: If the ear is deformed or some part is missing, this may cause speech handicap.
(5) *Carelessness in the development of speech*: If proper care is not taken by parents in early infancy, the speech defect may develop.
(6) Cerebral palsy and hurt in the brain.
(7) *Imitation of incorrect speech*: Children in early childhood may imitate defective speech in the company of their classmates and friends that results in defective speech.
(8) Deformation of mouth, teeth and palate.
(9) *Deep-seated Dysphasia*: Emotional conflicts in which the hesitant speech reflects an underlying anxiety which may cause speech handicap.
(10) Abnormal tonsils, cleft palate and obstruction in the nasal passage.
(11) *Paralysis of the tongue*: Paralysis of tongue stops the movement of the tongue and hence develops speech handicap.
(12) *Heredity*: In some cases, heredity may be the cause of speech handicap. If the father is a stutter, the son inherits naturally.

(13) Apraxia: It is a disorder in the ability to perform planned or voluntary muscle involvements, may not be able to move the mouth up and down for producing speech.

(14) Dysarthria: It is a collection of motor speech disorders where the muscles do not function properly due to damage to the nervous system (Nicobsi, 1989).

Problems of Speech Impairment

Children with impaired speech face many problems in daily life. Some important problems are discussed below:

(a) Maladjustment is very common among these children. There will be absence of functional or age appropriate communication systems. They show aggressive tendencies, anxieties and fears. They perceive their parents as authoritarian figures. They have been poor self-image.

(b) These children feel inferior to normal children. They are under achievers, whom generally do not conform to the general behaviour pattern.

(c) Sometimes other children make fun of their defective speech and consequently the child withdraws himself/herself from the social situation which results in poor the socialization and social interaction.

(d) Children often become conscious of their defects. They find difficulty in communicating with others. They cannot take active part in games and group activities, as the language disorder interferes with the quality of inter-personal relationships.

(e) A poor articulator is often poor in auditory discrimination. Pronunciation difficulties interfere with word recognition and spelling. This leads to poor learning and achievement in cognitive tasks.

Education Provisions

The speech-language pathologist plays an important role in diagnosing hearing problems and are responsible for fitting hearing aids. Speech-language pathologists identify, assess and provide treatment to children with speech/communication disorders. They also treat difficulties in speaking due to paralytic stroke or head injuries, stuttering, poor clarity in speech articulation, fluency voice problems. They also evaluate whether there is omissions substitutions additions and distortions of speech sounds. The following educational provisions can be made for speech-impaired children.

(1) ***Curriculum*****:** Curriculum for children with speech disorder should consider prevention, remediation and compensation. Efforts should be taken to prevent the occurrence by introducing proper speech pattern. Through remediation programme speech pattern should be corrected. And through compensatory intervention programme alternative skills are provided to them to communicate what they want to. Remediation interruptions try to change the pattern that is not correct or not functional.

(2) ***Speech Therapy*****:** If a child needs speech or language therapy, an expert or a therapist should be consulted. Very often the school does not have any facility for this purpose. In such cases, parents should be advised to contact the nearest speech and hearing center. The speech therapists help children in correcting and removing disabilities.

(3) ***Articulation Correction*****:** When parents are not in a position to obtain the required help for children, the resource teachers may help the child to do simple corrections in articulation.

(4) ***Speech Training Activities*****:** Teaching experts can make a more direct contribution by giving the child practice in using the correct sound after it has been elicited by the speech therapist.

(5) ***Extra Curricular Activities*****:** Besides the above, the children should be taken to visit places of interest, historical, social, cultural or geographical places, where they may ask some questions and answers given to them would help them learn new words.

(6) ***Role of Parents***: In western countries, parents are very conscious of the speech defects of their children. But it is not so in India. Parents should take care of the speech defects in their children, consult with speech and psychotherapists and try to be confident about their children's achievements. Early diagnosis and intervention will help the children come out from problem.

(7) ***Role of Teacher***: It is the primary duty of a teacher to understand the speech defects of the child under him/her. As the society neglects these children, the love and sympathy of the teacher can contribute a lot to help them improve the child's speech defects.

III. HEARING IMPAIRMENT

Pavitra, a three-year-old child, when called by her mother, responds slowly. She takes time to turn to her mother. Takes very little interest in listening to rhymes. The mother is worried. She takes the child to Pre-Primary school. The teacher asks few questions to Pavitra. She closely observes the teacher speaking and with repeated questioning only she answers. She has been then referred to an audiologist for a check up. He declares that child is hard of hearing. Hence she is not able to understand immediately when spoken, the audiologist suggests a therapy and few activities to be given to Pavitra so that she could be a successful child with her normal peer. Both parents and the teachers are now convinced that they have to accept their child's speech pattern and guide her without making her feel inferior, that she has hard of hearing whereas her friends are normal. This will enable to over come this hearing impairment gradually.

Hearing is the main sensory pathway through which speech and verbal communication develop. If a child hears imperfectly, he is likely to speak incorrectly. Again, hearing also influences learning and other aspects of maturation. Early detection of hearing impairment is important for the child's over-all development.

Definition

Hearing impairment has been defined by many. According to Streng "The hard of hearing are those with reducing hearing acuity either, since birth or acquired any time during life."

According to Fredrick S. Berg and Samuel G. Fletcher:

'The hard of hearing child is a hearing impaired individual who cannot identify through hearing and without receptive communication enough of the distinguishing features of speech to at least partial recognition of the spoken language. With the addition of visual receptive communication such as speech reading, he may understand more language provided the vocabulary and syntax are a part of his linguistic code.

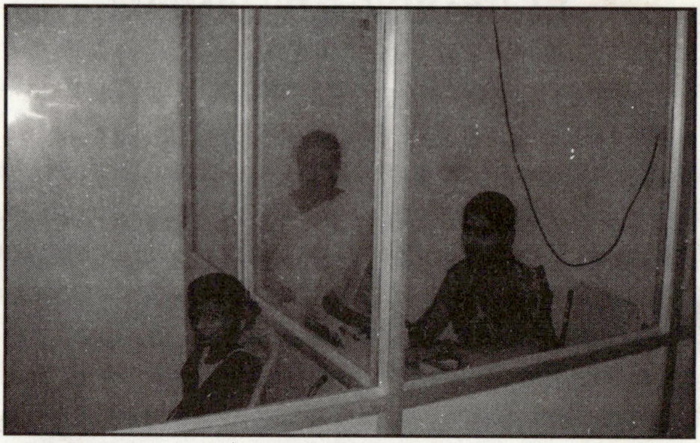

Audio Testing

Keeping Fit

Sign Method

Class Room Learning

Group Method

Direct Method

Learning Rhymes

Learning with Computer

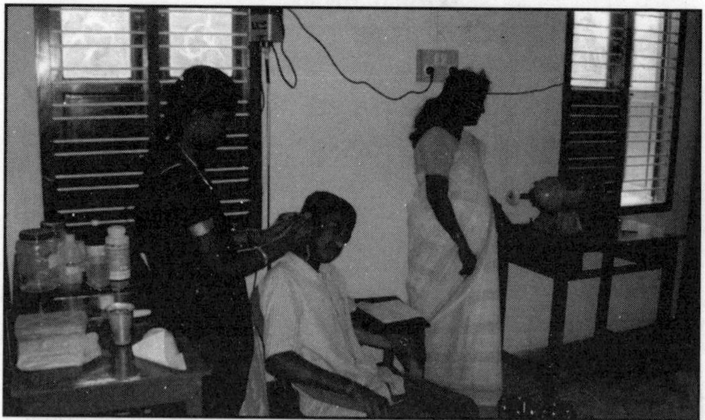

Preparing Ear Mould

Three terms—hearing impairment, deafness and hard of hearing or auditorily impaired. Hearing impairment implies the entire loss of hearing, mainly genetic in nature. Deafness refers to profound hearing loss. They are unable to perceive sounds in the environment with or without use of hearing aid and unable to use hearing as a way to gain information. Hard of hearing refers to significant hearing loss. They have sufficient, residual hearing but with hearing and they can comprehend others speech and oral communication.

Further it is also classified as pre-lingually deaf and post-lingually deaf. Pre-lingually deaf are those who are born deaf; lost the ability to hear before developing language. Post-lingually deaf are those who become deaf after birth due to injury, after developing language.

The partially hearing, are those who lose acuity of hearing severely and require a special educational curriculum and programme of training that involves full time auditory training along with vision for developing language and communication skills.

Causes of Hearing Impairment

Hearing impairment is generally caused by some defects in the ears. Various causes of have been attributed to this. Hearing loss occurs when some part of the outer, inner, or middle ear is not functioning properly. Hearing loss may be conducive or sensorineural. When the sound loss is not due to sound perception lent by sound can direction. Outer or middle ear is affected not the inner ear. Sensorineural, hearing loss or nerve deafness is caused by infection in the inner ear or along the nerve pathway from the inner ear to the brain.

1. **Hereditary:** The deafness may be due to hereditary factors. The deafness may be transmitted from generation to generation.
2. **Pre-natal causes**: Pre-natal infection and toxic conditions of the mother may cause hearing impairment. Mothers

who suffer from viruses of mumps and influenza in early pregnancy may cause degeneration of important nerve cells that results in deafness.

3. **Traumatic experiences at birth**: During delivery certain traumatic experiences such as pelvic pressure, use of forceps in delivery and internal haemorrhage may also cause damage to the nervous system resulting in auditory defects. Prolonged lack of oxygen due to prolonged labour; heavy sedation or blockage of the infants respiratory passage may also cause hearing defects in the children. Premature delivery followed by jaundice and use of anesthetic agents in delivery may also cause hearing problems.
4. **Causes after birth:** There are certain conditions, which may cause hearing defects such as:

(i) *Post-natal diseases*: Majority of hearing defects are caused by post-natal diseases such as scarlet fever, mumps, whooping coughs, typhoid fever and influenza.

(ii) *Accidents*: Accidents may also cause hearing loss. Hurt on certain parts of the head may also lead to hearing defects.

(iii) *Psychological causes*: Emotional depression and traumas may cause hearing problems. Soldiers develop hearing defects. In order to resolve a deep unconscious conflict during war.

(iv) *Old age*: In old age, hearing deterioration occurs.

Characteristics of Hearing Impaired

Children with the hearing lose exhibit the following characteristics:

1. **Difficulty in following directions**: If the students do not respond when spokes and do not follow the directions of the teacher, it means there is something wrong with the hearing of the students.

2. Turning head to one side to hear better: If a students frequently turns his/her head to one side to hear better, it also indicates that the student has some problem with hearing.

3. Not paying attention: If a student is inattentive and day-dreaming in the class, it means either she/he is not able to listen what the teacher says or he is not motivated to learn.

4. Hesitancy to participate in large groups: Hearing impaired child avoids group activity such as group games.

5. Colds accompanied with earaches: The student with hearing impairment frequently suffers with cold and earaches.

6. Problems in understanding speech: Does not understand speech.

7. In security: Stubborn withdrawal behaviour used to project feelings between observed ability of child and test scores. There is great discrepancy in his observed ability and test score.

8. Uses loud voice while speaking.

9. Gives incorrect answer to the questions.

10. Misarticulated certain sounds.

11. Shows restricted vocabulary when speaking.

12. Exhibits confused expression on face.

Identification of Hearing Impaired

Early identification and intervention is very essential for preventing speech and language defects of the hearing impaired, by adopting the following procedures.

1. Maintenance of High-risk Register

Volunteers trained by audiologist maintain a high-risk register. It contains:

(a) History of hereditary childhood hearing impairment.
(b) Fatal Diseases.
(c) Defects of ear, nose, throat.
(d) Birth weight (less than 1500 gems).

2. Screening Procedure

(a) *Behaviours observation*: The technique involves presentation of known fixed intensity sound when the child is asleep and sees whether he responds to it.

(b) *Crib gram*: It comprises a crib to the sides of which two speakers are connected, which are in turn connected to a sound source. Whenever the sound is produced, the child makes a movement. The movements are recorded.

Educational Provisions for Hearing Impaired

The crucial point of education of hearing impaired is to provide educational experiences that commensurate with their hearing peers with lot of usual experiences and in addition to provide necessary remedial and therapeutic programme in the areas of language and speech. Children with hearing impairment can be accommodated in the general classroom. Teacher should pay attention to the seating arrangement in the classroom without disturbing the visibility of the teachers. Teacher may also think of having a buddy system where there will be peer support.

Special attention is to be provided to develop vocational skills, needed for the children with hearing impairment.

1. Understanding oneself and others
2. Travelling allone when needed.
3. Health checks up.
4. Safety is to be ensured.
5. World of work is to be understood.
6. Home management—able to manage once requirement at home.
7. Money management—understand the value of money-currency and coins.
8. Motor development and physical activities in which special training is to be provided.

9. Fine Arts—appreciates and participates in other forms such as painting, dancing and handcrafts.
10. Citizenship responsibility.

1. Instructional strategies: With all the instructional procedures the following could be added.

2. Use of hearing aids: The hearing aid is very necessary for hearing impaired. Training in its use and care, usage of headphones etc. are useful training strategies for educating the hearing impaired. At the same time effective communication is to be ensured.

3. Auditory Training: Perception of various speech sounds is possible through this training. Discrimination of speech sounds, sign language lip reading, and speech development are a part of this training. Should use more gestures and facial expressions.

4. Speech Reading: This is on act of understanding a speaker without hearing just by watching the movement of lips and tongue. Teaching speech reading is a tedious job, which requires patience. Manual method and finger spelling help them understand and communicate.

5. Classroom arrangements: The hearing impaired should be front-benchers. The teacher should make use of a reasonable level of pitch. Lip-reading should be supplementary. Teacher must avoid moving while speaking, as they observe the lips and gestures of the teacher.

Review Questions

1. Describe briefly the types of sensory disabilities.
2. What are the causes of visual impairment?
3. Enumerate the points to be kept in mind while educating the visually impaired.
4. As a teacher how will you diagnose speech defects and suggest suitable remedial measures.
5. List and explain the types of
   (1) Visual impairment

(2) Aural impairment
(3) Speech impairment
(6) Identify the specific characteristics of children with speech defects
(7) In what way is aural impairment related to speech impairment?
(8) Describe suitable educational provisions for aurally impaired children.

4

Mentally Challenged

Manjula is a 15-year-old girl. But she depends on others to support her even for satisfying her immediate basic needs. She stares at people when they try to communicate with her. The parents feel very bad that they have such a daughter who depends on others for everything and she is growing up. They are worried about their daughter's future as well. As a psychologist what advice will you give to Manjula's parents? Will you allow Manju's parents just to worry about without taking any efforts to help her to take care of at least her basic requirements? What would be your guidance to Manju's parents?

Raju is an adult with severe mental retardation. He is left in the street without any care. Children make fun of him and throw stones at him. Sometimes they feed him also. As a social worker what will be your intervention at this stage of Raju? How will you help Raju? Have you seen any arrangement in the neighbourhood where such people are taken care of or some provision is made to teach them soft skills and social skills needed to deal with the people in the community? Is there a rehabilitation centre to take care of such children in the community?

Visit the institutions where arrangements are made for people with mentally retarded and study the different arrangements made to make them live on their own without depending on others even for taking care of themselves. Suggest what would be the ideal programme for Manju and Raju. In the following package we will learn more about mentally challenged, their care and education procedures to be adopted.

Mentally challenged are the people who have seriously impaired intellectual ability that affects their learning. They are also members of the family and society. They too experience all the emotions, joy, sorrows, sadness, love, pride, disappointment etc. like any human being. But mentally challenged seems to be a stigma and a negative concept, that remains a challenge to human race as a whole. As a matter of terminology, such children are known by so many other names such as, 'feeble-minded', 'mentally challenged', 'mentally deficient', 'mentally sub-normal' or 'mentally sub-average' or 'mentally retarded'. The inability of mentally challenged creates obstacles in their lives. They need to have support from families, friends, and teachers in the community so that they could overcome these obstacles. In this package effort is being made to make the learners understand.

Who are the mentally challenged children?
What are their specific characteristics?
What are their special requirements and what type of education is needed for them?

On completion of reading this package, the reader should be able to:

1. Define who is 'mentally challenged'?
2. List and explain the types of 'mentally retardation'.
3. Identify the causes of mentally retardation.
4. Enumerate the characteristics of mentally challenged.
5. Explain the test and non-test techniques for identifying mentally challenged.
6. Describe the educational provisions to be made for mentally challenged.

'Mental deficiency' is a state of incomplete mental development that the individual is incapable of adopting herself/ himself to the normal environment of his fellows, to maintain an existence independently without supervision, control or external supports. Mental deficiency has been defined in several ways. A few definitions of mental retardation or mentally challenged are discussed hereunder.

Mental retardation is a social construct that reflects the societal expectations of individuals with intellectual limitations where an individual is not able to fulfil the requirements of the society due to his/her limited intellectual ability.

Page (1976): defines, "Mental retardation is a condition of sub-normal mental development, present at birth or early childhood and characterized mainly by limited intelligence and social inadequacy."

According to ***Benda*** (1954) "A mentally defective person is a person who is incapable of managing himself and her/his affairs, or being taught of to do so and who requires supervision, control and care for his own welfare and the welfare of the community."

American Association on Mental Deficiency (1983): Mental retardation according to (American Association of Mental Retardation) AAMR: "refers to limitations in present functioning. It is characterized by significantly sub-average intellectual functioning existing concurrently with related limitations in two or more of the following applicable adaptive skill areas: Communication, self-care, home living, social skills community use, self-direction, health and safety, functional academics, leisure and work. Mental retardation manifests before (age) 18 (Luckasson *et al.* 1992).

Mental retardation is a social construct, which reflects the societal expectations of individuals with intellectual limitations. AAMR defines: "Mental retardation means significantly sub-average general intellectual functioning existing concurrently with deficits in adaptive behaviour and manifested during the developmental period that adversely affects a child's educational performance."

Let us try to analyze the viewpoints expressed in the above definitions. All these definitions agree that:

(1) Mentally challenged is a condition/state of mind.
(2) It is related to the sub-normal development of mind/brain/ intelligence.

(3) The deficiency may be observed at birth or manifested later during the course of development, generally before the end of the years of adolescence—18 years.

(4) The mentally challenged could be diagnosed through their very low scores on some standardized intelligence tests, the observation of their behaviour in the developmental period demonstrating impaired intellectual functioning, their inadequacy to deal with the demands of environmental and deficiency and defects in adaptive behaviour and mentally retarded are poor in their adaptive behaviour/skills-communication, social skills, self-care and functional academics.

Classification of Mentally Challenged Children

Mentally challenged are classified on the basis of their (i) Physical characteristics, (ii) Degree of retardation, (iii) Degree of independence, (iv) I.Q., and (v) Rate of Learning.

1. Classification on the basis of Physical Characteristics

Mentally challenged children have been categorized as under according to their physical and physiological capabilities and development. Mostly this relates to their intelligence, adaptive skills and need for support.

(i) Brain damage: This is an organic retardation, which occurs due to damage of the brain or because of some other sickness.

(ii) Mongoloid: These children can be recognized by their physical attributes like slanting eyes, flat nose, small sized head, broad head etc. Although friendly, modest and jolly they do often manifest obstinate behaviour too.

(iii) Cretin Child: This is also a condition of retardation. It occurs due to disturbance in thyroid glands. It can be cured at the primary stage, if identified early.

(iv) Phenylketonuria (PKU): This is found very rarely. PKU happens due to metabolic disturbances. When any poisonous matter enters into the brain through the blood circulation and destroys the brain cells PKU occurs.

(v) Microcephaly and Hydrocephaly: In this disorder the cerebrospinal fluid stops and the brain is either enlarged or remains small.

(vi) Cerebral Palsy: This is also a sort of brain damage. Some muscular activities become uncontrolled and such children's muscular adjustment becomes defective.

2. Classification on the basis of Degree of Retardation

Some psychologists and sociologists classify mentally challenged children according to the degree of retardation, as:

(i) Mildly Retarded or Challenged: The intellectual level of mildly retarded or challenged children remains under developed and it can be experienced at their school stage. They can be trained and improved up to some extent.

(ii) Moderately Challenged or Retarded: These children differ in their level of retardation, and it is visible during infancy. They learn to speak, walk or read very late and have less ability to grasp what is taught. They can be trained in motor skills.

(iii) Severely Retarded or Challenged: The brain of such children is totally disturbed. They are helpless in doing their daily household work and cannot be even trained to take care of themselves. They need some one to help them to take care even the physical requirements.

3. Classification on the basis of Degree of Independence

Sociologists have classified mentally challenged children into three groups, on the basis of their ability to take care of their personal needs.

(i) *Independent*: Those who can do their own work without any help from others.
(ii) *Partially independent*: Those who can do their daily routine work and want help for specific work.
(iii) *Dependent*: One who depends completely upon others for everything.

4. Classification on the basis of Intelligent Quotient (IQ) (Intellectual capability)

Mentally challenged children are classified on the basis of IQ by the psychologists. The classification on the basis of IQ is as follows:

I.Q.	*Classification*
Idiot	0-25
Imbecile	25-50
Moron	50-75
Dull	75-90
Average	90-110
Superior	110-125
Very Superior	125-140
Genius	140 and above

5. Classification on the basis of Rate of Learning—Adaptive Skill

On the basis of the rate of learning which helps the educators and parents, strategies of teaching and training are planned. The children are classified into four groups on the basis of their learning skills:

AAMR 1988 Classification	*IQ Range*	*Educational Classification*
Mild mental retardation or challenged	50-55 to 70	Slow learners or Educable
Moderate mental retardation or challenged	35-40 to 50-55	Trainable
Severe mental retardation or challenged	20-25 to 35-40	Severely/multiply handicapped
Profound mental retardation or challenged	Below 20 to 25	Severely/multiply handicapped

Mentally challenged lack self-direction, i.e., the ability to live their lives, difficulty in problem solving and making their own decisions. They are also poor in functional academic programmes such as filling an application form, to use a map or telephone directory, in learning words which are essential for survival in day-to-day life words like man/woman, enter/exit, stop/caution etc. poor in carrying out conversation and identification of denominations of money.

(i) *Educable Slow Learner*: Children with mild retardation are considered partially mentally retarded because their intellectual ability and efficiency remain below that of normal children. The difference is particularly in speed with which they learn. Their IQ remains between 50 and 75, so they are termed retarded. Most educationists include the children of 50 to 75 range of IQ in this group. Their physique develops like other normal children but they can be recognized on the basis of disorders in their motor skills and by physiological disorders in early childhood. Their retardation becomes visible during their schooling.

(ii) *Trainable*: The children of 35 to 50 IQ range are included under this category. Their motor development is very slow in their infancy and childhood and can be recognized on the basis of their physical structure. Their language development and behavioural efficiency also develop very late.

(iii) *Severe mental retardation.* Children with an IQ of 20 to 40 come under this category. They have multiple handicaps; including improper development of body and motor skills.

(iv) *Totally uneducable and unattainable*: Children with profound mental retardation come under this category. Their IQ range is less than 25 and the amount of retardation is very high. They are different in physique, body and locomotion from their childhood. They cannot learn through education and cannot even be made self-dependent.

In general MR lack intellectual capacity, capacity to learn, difficulty in distinguishing and paying attention to cues in social situations and attending to several cues simultaneously. When you give instruction more than one at a time, they will not be able to carry out. They also have poor memory, especially short-term memory to recall information that has been learnt a few seconds back. MR find difficulty in generalisation, i.e. the ability to transfer knowledge learnt from one task to another and there is lack of motivation in MR. Hence, they face frequent failure and exhibit low goal setting behaviour.

Causes of Mental Retardation

There are numerous reasons for mental retardation. It is difficult to say definitely which one factor is responsible for the retardation. The main causes can be divided into three categories as: (1) Parental factors, (2) Pre-natal factors and (3) Post-natal factors.

1. Parental factors

A few imbecile prone factors exist in parents before pregnancy in one of the spouses either or mother which affects the unborn child such as Down syndrome, Phenylketonuria PKU and maternal malnutrition. These factors are further categorized in the following ways:

(i) *Toxic Agents*: Poisonous material is produced by infection in the mother and is responsible for defective development of the child. For example, if the mother suffers from German measles, virus infection, typhoid etc. during pregnancy the child's mental development is affected.

(ii) *Drugs*: A few drugs enter accidentally in the reproductive organs of mother like carbon monoxide, LSD, and heroin; affect child's central nervous system. Drugs taken at the time of pregnancy, consumption of alcohol, and smoking by mothers, premature birth of fetus etc. affects the mental development of the child.

(iii) *Radiation*: Exposure to too much radiation during pregnancy causes retardation. Tension, high blood pressure, diabetes also affect the unborn child's mental development. Besides, a few blood defects, like ABO and RH factors also affect intellectual development.

The above three are biomedical causes developed within the individual.

(iv) *Genetics and Metabolism*: Due to defective genes of the parents retardation occurs. Ex: Mongolism. Various metabolic factors are also responsible for mental retardation. Fanlike-Urea is a metabolic defect. Its base is hereditary and continues in the family. This is also called as chromosomal disorder. At the time of conception itself this disorder occurs.

(v) *Physical and Mental Health of the Mother*: The mother's physical health, improper diet, unbalanced mental state, are some other causes of mental retardation of the child. Any serious damage that destroys the brain of the embryo causes defective mental development.

2. Pre-natal Factors

A few environmental factors also affect the brain and the child becomes mentally retarded. These are of three categories. (i) Prcmature Birth, (ii) Meningitice and (iii) Complications during delivery, like Head trauma at birth.

(i) *Premature Birth*: There are chances of children becoming mentally challenged if they are born during incomplete pregnancy or prematurely. It may also be due to any reproduction accident. The child's central nervous system is damaged and it can become a cause of abnormality and sometimes leading to death.

(ii) *Complications during delivery*: Complications arising during delivery sometimes cause mental retardation. A complicated delivery or operations are effective factors in causing mental retardation. The brain cells die at the time of birth due to insufficient intake of oxygen, and cannot be restored later on. Some kind of shock at the time of birth also affects the central nervous system and leads to mental retardation.

3. Post-natal Factors

The factors affecting mental development of a child after birth are categorized as: (i) Acute illness, (ii) Traumatic illness, (iii) Accidental Brain Injury, (iv) Lead Poisoning, and (v) Deprived Environment.

(i) *Acute Illness*: Some acute illness like typhoid, measles, pox, jaundice, whooping cough etc., in the post-natal period affect the child's mental development. Measles is an infectious disease, which damages the brain cells permanently.

(ii) *Traumatic Illness*: In this, the brain is damaged totally and the central nervous system is affected.

(iii) *Accidental Brain Injury;* Sometimes an accidental injury to the brain and disorders of the internal glands damage the nervous system.

(iv) *Lead Poisoning*: Sometimes the child consumes lead paints or wood paint by mistake or ignorance that causes mental retardation.

(v) *Deprived Environment*: One of the important causes of mental retardation is the low socio-economic and/or cultural status of the child. This includes malnutrition, unclean atmosphere, unhygienic conditions, insufficient resources for intellectual development, low education or illiteracy of parents, siblings, friend's etc. Cultural backgrounds too cause MR. These children with MR cannot adjust to any environment. For example, a child from a superstitious family will have faith in ghosts, and

may not accept the use of machines and may not adjust in a well-educated and cultured family. This may also lead to mental retardation and behavioural difficulties.

Characteristics of Mentally Retarded

Mental retardation can be identified through a few characteristics easily observed in other than normal children. The following are some of the characteristics: (1) Organic, (2) Physical, (3) Mental, (4) Educational, (5) Personal, Social and (6) Occupational Characteristics.

1. Organic Characteristics

(i) These children are similar to normal children. By their physical defects they can be identified.
(ii) They have physical disabilities like deafness and dumbness, hearing and speech disorder, blindness, brain injury and impairment of muscular adjustment.

2. Physical Characteristics

Physical characteristics of children with mental retardation are: they generally unhealthy and the IQ of their parents is also low. They belong to low socio economic status where they are deprived of a healthy atmosphere at home and environmental facilities are also very poor.

3. Mental Characteristics

(i) Such children are intellectually abnormal having an IQ range of 75 or below.
(ii) Due to a low IQ, they have a low maturation level and cannot do even an average work.
(iii) They have poor memory, generalization, conceptualization, perception, language ability, imagination and other activities demanding functional abilities.

4. *Educational Characteristics*

(i) Educationally these children with mental retardation are backward by two or three years as compared to normal children.
(ii) They are unable to grasp the lesson in a normal classroom and require special education.
(iii) They can learn to read, write and solve only simple mathematical problems.
(iv) They will not be able to learn higher educational concepts when they have greater degree of retardation.

5. *Personal and Social Characteristics*

(i) Mentally challenged children have a short attention span, which enables them to take interest only in limited activities.
(ii) They lack concentration and creativity.
(iii) Psychologically they are immature and have less tolerance and easily frustrated.
(iv) They can only repeat behaviour learnt from the neighbours or family members and may not be able to do anything on their own.
(v) They can take part in-group activities, play etc. with children of a lower age group.
(vi) Behaviour problems are common among children who are mentally challenged.

6. *Occupational Characteristics*

(i) Mentally challenged children will not be able to do highly skilled work due to intellectual deficiency.
(ii) They can be trained to do semi-skilled jobs.
(iii) They can do unskilled work or physical labour and social performance only.

Identification of Mentally Challenged Children

It is very important to identify mentally challenged as in scientific approach. The children can be identified on the basis of their performance in intelligent tests, various activities, achievement and minute observation of their work etc. A few important tests are: (1) Sanguine Form Board Test. (2) J. Bharat Raj: Development Screening Test. (3) R.P. Srivatsava and Kiran Saxena Mental Ability Test for 7 to 11 years. (4) C.M. Bhatia: Performance Intelligence Test Battery. (5) Malin: Weschler Intelligence Scale for Indian children.

Composition of these tests are described below:

(i) *Picture vocabulary Test*: These tests are used for children who have average hearing , vision and speaking abilities.

(ii) *Verbal and Non-verbal Tests of Mental Ability*: Determination of retardation cannot be achieved only by marks scored in the mental ability tests. Because sometimes other inefficiencies like culture, language etc., may also affect the special manifestation of the child. Therefore, a combination of verbal, non-verbal as well as performance tests should be used to measure IQ of children.

(iii) *Drawing Test*: Through 'Draw a Man Tests' the scores are obtained by drawing the full picture of a man on outlines of models. The retardation of the child can be assessed, on the basis of number of parts of the body correctly drawn in the outline given.

(iv) *Tests of perceptual measures*: These are also used to observe different perceptual abilities.

Educating the Mentally Challenged

Three major types of mentally challenged children have been identified by using observation of their behaviour in social context and administering performance objective tests and other standardized intelligence tests.

1. Dependent Mentally challenged
2. Educable Mentally challenged
3. Trainable Mentally challenged

1. Curriculum for Dependent Mentally Challenged

Dependent mentally challenged children are those who depend on others for their survival and are not able to work independently throughout their lives, including their personal care.

The following eight areas are identified and included in the curriculum of totally dependent mentally challenged, such as Motor Skills, Self-care Programme, Communication, Concept formation, Socialization, Purposeful activity, Travelling and Leisure/Fine Arts etc.

Principles of teaching the dependent mentally challenged children:

1. *Supervision and care*: Supports of the staff is needed to give medical treatment and health care to the mentally challenged children.
2. *Mobility*: Staff and physical supports are required because of physical handicap or blindness, to move around.
3. *Socialization, Communication*: The number of staff and programme supports are needed to ensure that personal routine activities such as eating, dressing, toileting are carried out, by the children who are mentally challenged.
4. *Developmental skills*: The staff and programme supports are needed to ensure that personal routines such as eating, dressing, toileting are carried out.
5. *Behaviour*: The intensity of staff and programme supports are needed for control and training where the behaviour problems, of mentally challenged children, are vigorous and acute.

Types of Special Education Programme

1. Residential Schools

Children who are mentally challenged should be kept in well-equipped hospital-*cum*-schools. Capable and specially trained nurses and doctors should be appointed to take care of them. Those children who cannot do their daily chores need to live in such institutes, as they depend on others for everything, including eating, toileting etc.

2. Special Schools

The special schools are considered very practical and more beneficial to those children who are educable. The child goes to school for a fixed time only and makes social progress too. The division of class in these schools should be made on the basis of requirements, level of ability and age. There should be provision for relaxation and rest in school. The special services of trained teachers, nurses and social workers should be made available to them, to provide guidance and counselling along with giving instructions in functional skills.

3. Special Classes

Arrangement of special classes in the general school is made where proper education for MR and training facilities are available. During the rest of the time they stay with normal children. This arrangement is defective from the disciplinary point of view. A separate homogenous class system is more effective, for children who are mentally challenged. We could decide which type will be suitable only after assessing the child's degree of mental retardation.

2. Education of the Educable Mentally Challenged

The mental age of educable retarded children is generally lower than the average children. Hence, an appropriate curriculum according to the degree of retardation is to be planned so that they can have full benefit.

1. Curriculum

Retarded children cannot derive benefit from fixed curriculum, meant for normal children, hence an appropriate curriculum according to their needs and mental age should be adopted. It should have remedial component, along with general classroom support to make them more independent in acquiring functional academic programme.

At the Primary level the main object of the curriculum is to provide self- care, promote harmony, manipulation of object, learn to respect, co-operate, and help to promote speech between 3 and 8 years of age.

Training in adaptive skills such as wearing clean clothes, toilet training, choral singing, pronunciation etc. should also be developed.

2. Middle Level Curriculum

In the middle level (6 to 18 years) the curriculum for MR, should include reading, writing, and mathematics. Training in semi-skilled and unskilled jobs should also be given. They are to be taught to engage themselves in games, dramatics, arts, handicraft, music etc.

3. Curriculum for Adults

People with very low IQ up to the age of 25 years need some vocational ability and skills to do things on their own. Hence some vocational courses should be included in the curriculum. They should also be provided with knowledge on their responsibility towards themselves, their family and the community. Adults thus are to be trained in vocational and social skills besides acquiring basic skills.

Strategies of Curriculum Transaction

1. Periods of short duration

Mentally retarded/challenged have short period and short span attention and concentration.

So formal-teaching periods should be kept fairly short. It is of importance to note as to how long a child can concentrate when the subject is taught and while fixing the duration of a class period, care should be taken whether the subject stimulates the child and sustains his/her interest.

2. Repetition

As the memory span of such children is very short, the materials and methods of instruction should be interesting and motivate the children learn. Repetition is a must for these children.

3. Projects

'Introduction of projects' or 'centers of interest' is a significant approach for teaching mentally challenged children. The teachers should teach that arise out of natural classroom situations. The point of origin may be a short story, a poem, a song or a picture or an activity or an experience of the child. Undue importance should not be given to the source, but the teachers must know how to present it through careful planning and guidance, so that the child gets real involvement in learning and participates in the learning process with willingness.

3. Education of the Trainable Mentally Challenged

The trainable mentally challenged children have IQ, which ranges from 25-55. They are much more retarded than the educable mentally retarded. In their curriculum, less emphasis is given to teaching of academic subjects and more time is devoted to development of daily living skills and social skills. The curriculum thus should include:

Self care activities, social training, sensory training, learning language skills, crafts and music.

(1) Self-care Activities: This is a programme of simple habit formation like eating, bathing, dressing and toilet training. This enables the children to develop skills of self-help in respect of their daily practical needs. Methods, which are adopted for this purpose, should relate to experiences and everyday needs of children.

(2) Social Training: Priority should be given to group activities such as group games, simple dramatic work and story-telling etc. This may increase the gregariousness and affiliation. The children become generally active, co-operative, and learn to adjust with others in the home and community.

(3) Sensory Training: Special emphasis must be laid on instructions by which the children will be able to make the fullest use of their senses. As sensory organs are the gateways of learning it is essential that children with intellectual deficiency are given opportunities to get trained in using their sensory organs properly.

(4) Communicative Ability: Mentally challenged children must be provided with some aids and opportunities through which they can have better speech development and proper understanding of verbal concepts. Unless they are trained to communicate properly learning new concepts will be difficult. Proper communication, including conversation with others alone will make the child a social being.

(5) Craft-work and Music: For developing the feeling of self-confidence in these children with mental disability, the curriculum should include simple work experience or crafts like weaving, rug making, basket making, painting etc. should be taught. By having this economic self-sufficiency can be achieved. Learning music and playing with others make them become soft. Children should also be trained in learning to complete a job application form, learning to use a city map or telephone directory, learning the common terms in everyday life situations, learning to carry on a reciprocal conversation and learning to identify denomination of coins and currencies.

Prevention of Mental Retardation

If we take some measures to prevent the preventable causes the number of children with mental retardation could be reduced. There

Mentally Challenged

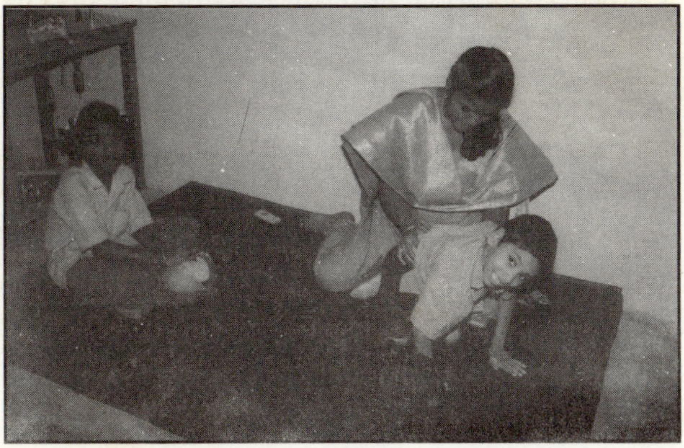

Physiothera

are three elements in prevention of mental retardation; Primary prevention refers to intervention before the cause occurs like bio-medical or psychosocial problems which include vaccines for the prevention of diseases like rubella, awareness creation on drug abuse by pregnant women and prenatal testing such as amniocentesis.

Secondary prevention refers to intervention immediately after diagnosing primary causes of MR. Tertiary prevention refers to special education and physical, occupational or vocational training to reduce the effects of a disability. Critical areas of prevention also includes; lack of prenatal care, infant mortality, low birth weight, adolescent pregnancy and child bearing, poor nutrition, environmental or toxic exposures, sexually transmitted diseases including pediatric HIV and AIDS, injuries, child abuse and neglect, lack of early intervention and other biomedical considerations.

If the above steps are taken mental retardation could be prevented and the problems of mentally challenged will be reduced to a considerable extent.

Review Questions

1. Define 'mentally challenged' and give its classification.
2. Enumerate the various factors that cause mental retardation.
3. Describe the various characteristics of mentally challenged children.
4. Analyze the use of testing-techniques to identify mentally challenged.
5. Describe the various educational provisions available for mentally challenged children.
6. Suggest a suitable curriculum for mentally challenged children at the primary level.
7. Do you agree with providing inclusive education to children with mentally challenged? If so to which type and at what level?

5

Giftedness

For a good part of history of man has been searching for new and more appropriate terms by which to designate persons with intellectual exceptionalities. One among such category is the 'intellectually gifted'. The other two being, the creative and the mentally challenged. Intellectually gifted are those whose performance in a potentially valuable line of human activity is consistently remarkable. These children are not benefited by normal classroom teaching in school because the teaching in general class does not motivate them for learning, it is below their intellectual capacity. This package deals with the meaning, various concepts related to the gifted and various educational procedures to be followed.

Learning Objectives

On completion of reading this package, the reader will be able to

(1) Define: Who is a gifted child and the relationship between giftedness and its relationship with intelligent quotient?
(2) Explain the methods of identifying gifted children.
(3) Identify the gifted children.
(4) List and explain the characteristics of gifted children.
(5) Describe the educational provisions for gifted children.

Two year old Saranya does all her reading and writing at home even without attending the school or without any formal education. She has been barred from school because of her underage. Saranya, who can read and write fluently without any problem has to wait for 15 more months before she steps into a school despite her exceptional progress, in 3 Rs—Reading, Writing and Arithmetic.

The Education Act in our country permits admission of any child into a formal school only on the basis of his chronological age and not on his intellectual age. As per the rule a child could be admitted into first standard only on completion of 5 years of age. This is the case of many bright children in the world which leads to the wastage of many intellectual exceptionalities and their early contributions to the world. But, thanks to a few schools which smoothen this situation by identifying the gifted children either at the time of entering the school or when they face some problems with this type of children at home itself.

Who is a Gifted Child?

Definition of the term gifted is somewhat ambiguous and imprecise in the psychological literature. According to R.J. HaVinghust, "gifted children are those individuals, from Kindergarten through high school age, who show unusual promise in some socially useful area and whose talent might be stimulated."

John White (1970) summarised the characteristics of gifted child as, "a child is labelled gifted as she/he either he has a high IQ or has a very high score on a so called creativity test or he shows at an early age to me specific ability in mathematics, music, painting or social leadership".

In psychology, there are no hard and fast lines to separate one group from another. Anyhow, Psychologists have defined the 'very superior' and the 'gifted' groups in terms of intelligence quotients.

IQ	*Percentage in Population*
160 and above	0.03
150-159	0.2 (Gifted)
140-149	1.1
130-139	3.1 (Very superior)

Gifted, therefore are those children whose cognitive abilities place them in the upper level of population distribution. They constitute only 3 to 5 per cent of the population. The academically gifted has an IQ of 130 and above. They have superior cognitive ability, creativity in thinking and production and superior talent in special areas.

According to Guilford,"gifted are those students whose potential intellectual powers are at such a high ideational level in both productive and evaluative thinking that it can be reasonably assumed, that they could be the future problem solvers, innovators and evaluators of the culture if provide adequate educational experiences and opportunities".

According to the Act of 1978 (Educational Amendments of 1978) the definition of giftedness is as follows:

"Gifted and talented children means children, and whenever applicable, youth, who are identified at the pre-school, elementary or secondary level as possessing, demonstrated or potential activities that give evidence of high performance capability in areas such as intellectual, creative, specific academic or leadership ability, or in the performing and visual arts, and who by reason thereof require services or activities not ordinarily provided by the school."

Now, 'giftedness' is also called as outstandingly talented and exceptionally talented'.

Causes of Giftedness

We usually attribute giftedness to the nature (genetic factors) and nurture (psychological factors) of the child. There is a perspective that "giftedness is a biologically rooted concept, a label for a high level of intelligence that results from the advanced and accelerated integration of function with the brain, including physical sensing, emotions, cognition and information" (Clark, 1920). This concept justifies the role of nature and nurture.

The following could also be the probable causes for giftedness, which are external in nature:

(1) Excellent and conducive atmosphere at home and friends;

(2) Early and excellent opportunity for experiences and experiments;
(3) Early and excellent and continuous guidance and instruction;
(4) Opportunity to practice and express talents and progress according to their ability;
(5) Close association with others of the same ability;
(6) Opportunities for accomplishment within their capabilities with increasing challenges;
(7) Provision and opportunity for strong success and recognition of successes.

The Concept of Mental Age and IQ

While defining 'giftedness', we have been mentioning the term 'IQ'. What is IQ? Intelligence is assessed through various intelligence tests in terms of IQ (or) Intelligence Quotient. This term was first coined by William Stern. The formula for calculation of IQ is:

$$IQ = \frac{MA}{CA} \times 100$$

MA stands for Mental Age
CA for Chronological Age

The concept of mental age was first introduced by French Psychologist Alfred Binet in 1905 itself. It was based on the principle of the normal distribution of intelligence that the majority of children of a particular age are of normal intelligence and that they have a mental level approximating that age, which could be termed as their mental age. If some child excels in the performance of a certain task compared to the performance of the majority of children of his/her age, he/she was said to be of a higher mental age. If, for instance, the performance of an eight year old on certain adequately determined tasks is equal to that of a majority of ten-year old, then he/she has a mental age of ten year, whereas another child of eight years showing performance equal to that of the majority of 6 years old, on the same tasks would said to possess a mental age of 6 years.

For example, if the mental age of a 10-year old child is 12, his IQ is:

$$IQ = \frac{12}{10} \times 100 = 120$$

Charateristics of Gifted Children

Although there are individual differences among gifted children, still there are certain common characteristics. Different psychological studies have revealed some of the following characteristics of gifted children.

(a) *Physique and Health*: Generally gifted children are slightly physically superior. They recognise the value of sleep, play and good food habits.
(b) *School Achievement*: Most gifted children like school and usually they are high achivers.
(c) *Reading Development*: They can read quickly, safely and their performance is better than other children.
(d) *Interests*: Giftedness is characterised by enthusiasm and gifted children are interested in activity. They usually persist in the face of difficulty.
(e) *Social and Emotional Development*: Gifted children possess a high organizing capacity, which influences their emotional development. They, generally, are emotionally stable but become aggressive and challenge the authority on situation that are unreasonable.
(f) *Character and Personality*: A majority of gifted children show superiority in character and personality. They excel in rapidity in learning and remembering, the ability to analyze, reasoning, reproducing already learnt etc. They have the power of sustained attention.

The characteristics of giftedness could thus be summaraised as follows:

(1) Exhibit high sensitivity.
(2) Have excessive energy.
(3) Get bored easily and appear to have short attention spans.
(4) Would like to have emotionally stable and secure adults around them.
(5) Resist authority.
(6) Have their own preference for ways of reading and mathematics.
(7) Easily frustrated if their wish is not fulfilled.
(8) Preference for explorative learning and not rote memory or merely to be a passive listener.
(9) Cannot sit still unless active and interesting.
(10) Very compassionate and have fears of death, and loss of dear ones.
(11) Will give up learning if they experience failure at an early stage.
(12) Show high academic ability.
(13) Exhibit creative and productive thinking.
(14) Display well developed social skills and leadership ability.

Identification of Gifted Children

One of the important problems concerning the education of gifted children is identifying them from in general population. Dunlop commenting on the procedure of identifying gifted children remarked, 'no one method provides adequate identification of all children with high mental ability. Teachers' judgements based on individual characteristics and classroom intelligence and achievement tests and all findings substantiated by individual tests'.

Methods of identifying giftedness can be classified under two broad categories, as Test techniques and Non-test techniques.

A. Test Techniques

As we know that giftedness is linked with IQ score, the use of some form of intelligence test would seem obvious. These tests can be broadly classified as follows: Individual tests in which only one individual is tested at a time. Group tests in which a group of individuals is tested at the same time.

This could further be classified as Verbal or language tests and Non-verbal or non-language tests.

Verbal or Language Tests: make use of language in which the instructions are given in words, written, oral or both. The individuals being tested are required to use language, verbal or written while responding.

Non-Verbal or Non-Language Tests: involve activities in which the use of language is not needed except for giving directions.

(i) Individual Verbal Tests

(a) The French Psychologist Alfred Binet, along with Theodore Simon prepared an intelligent test in 1905, consisting of 30 items (arranged in order of increasing difficulty) graded for different age levels.

(b) The Binet test has been adopted in India also by many. The first such attempt was made by C.H. Rice in 1922 when he published his 'Hindustani Binet Performance Point Scale'. This was an adoptation of Binet test with some additional performance tests.

(c) The state 'Manovigyanshala' of Uttar Pradesh has made a Hindi version of StanfordBinet test.

(ii) Individual Non-Verbal Tests

(a) Block building or cube construction: The subject is asked to make a structure or design by means of cubes/blocks supplied to him/her. This Merril Palmer Block Building, Koch's Block Design test etc. are examples of test involving this type of activity.

(b) To fit blocks in holes: Test material of this type provides numerous blocks and a board on which there are holes, which correspond to the shape and size of these blocks.

The subject has to fit the blocks in the corresponding holes. **There are also other types of tests like Maze test and Picture Completion test:**

(c) *Tracing a Maze*: Here the subject has to trace with a pencil, the path from entrance to exit in a maze, which ranges from simple to complex.

(d) *Picture Completion Test*: A group of such tests are available through which we could obtain a comprehensive idea of a person's mental ability. Some well known scales are: The Pinter-Patterson scale, The Arthur Point scale and Alexander's Battery of Performance Tests.

(iii) Group Verbal Tests

The tests which necessitate the use of language and are applied to a group of individuals at a time or simultaneously come under this category. CIE verbal group test of intelligence (Constructed by Prof. Uday Shankar), The group test of General Mental Ability *(Samuhik Mansik Yogyata Pariksha)* constructed by S. Jalota and Army Alpha Test (developed during World War I).

(iv) Group Non-Verbal Intelligence Tests

These test do not necessitate the use of language. The subject is expected to perform tests only and are applicable to a group of individuals at a time.

Some examples of Group tests are:

(i) ***Army Beta Test*:** This was developed during World War I in the USA for testing the intelligence of soldiers who were either illiterates or not familiar with the English language.

(ii) ***Chicago-Non-verbal Test*:** This non-verbal test has proved most useful for young children aged 12 and 13 years.

(iii) ***Raven's Progressive Matrices Test*:** This test was developed in United Kingdom. This test has been designed to evaluate the subjects ability: (a) to see the relationship between geometric figures or designs, and (b) to perceive the structures of a design in order to select the appropriate part for completion of each pattern.

B. Non-Test Techniques

- **(i)** ***Using Pupil Attainment*:** This method is to use attainment of a child as shown in school record cards.
- **(ii)** ***Identification by Teachers*:** Teachers can play an important role in the process of identification of gifted children, through their periodical observation and interaction in the class room and outside the school environment.

***Observation*:** The teacher can study through observation, the behavioural characteristics of gifted children. The teacher should observe the academic and non-academic activities of gifted children, not only inside the classroom but also their behaviour with others, the elders, the peer group etc.

(a) Academic: The gifted child may show exceptional progress in one or more areas of the curriculum. The teacher should therefore look for underlying abilities rather than attainment.

- (i) The teacher must remain alert for the explosion of activity that may follow when some topic suddenly inspires a child's imagination and curiosity.
- (ii) The gifted child often has good memory and capable of processing complex information.
- (iii) Gifted children will finish their work very rapidly and spend much time in day-dreaming or secretly reading the book hidden under the desk.
- (iv) Advanced reading ability and verbal fluency are also good indications of giftedness. These children have longer span of attention than normal children and enjoying working independently.
- (v) Gifted children seem to have a much more clearer conception of themselves and definite notions of their goals.

(b) Non-Academic:

(i) The identifiction of children's hobbies can often provide useful information regarding child's potential. Here the teacher should keep in his/her mind that it is not only the interest but the intensity and persistence of the interest taken in it.

(ii) All gifted children have a good sense of humour.

(iii) Teacher should also observe children, while engaged in extracurricular activities like drama, debates, games, picnics etc., where they could exhibit their various talents.

Educational Practices

Teaching the gifted children needs extra efforts. In fact it is a challenge to the teachers to keep these children engaged fully. Educational practices can be followed be dealt under two broad headings, as (a) Administrative arrangement for gifted children, and (b) Teaching strategies for gifted children.

A. Administrative Arrangements

After identifying the gifted children we could make the following arrangements. There are three types of administrative arrangements which are generally made for the education of gifted children. They are, Ability Grouping, Acceleration, Enrichment and Integrated education.

(i) Ability Grouping

Ability grouping is segregation of gifted children from normal children and make it a homogeneous group. This method p des opportunity to include extra subject matter and special classes, greater depth of knowledge, more enrichment, more suitable teaching methods and more time for teachers to provide individual guidance according to their interest and capability. There are several variations of ability grouping.

(a) *Special Schools*: In special schools for gifted children there are special arrangements for maximum developments of their academic and vocational skills. The Navodaya Vidyalaya, which is also called space setting school, aims at such all-round excellence of these gifted children. More and varied opportunities are provided to learn on their own.

(b) *Special Class*: This method is the formal seggregation arrangement for educating the gifted with the same subject matter as that of normal children but it differs in the depth of examination and the range of supporting activities. Gifted will have to examine differently with more concepts, experiments etc. than the average children.

(c) *Differentiated programme*: The differentiated programme on multiple-track plan is a very old and very common one. Students are not put in special classes except where these classes are required as a part of the programme leading to a particular diploma.

(d) *Core and special classes*: Arguments against homogenous grouping are sometimes met by allowing all students take certain courses together and students with higher intellectual capacity take special subjects to learn on their own.

(e) *Released time*: The released time approach has usually been coupled with a system of seminars debate etc. The assumption is that able students can accomplish generally required tasks in an abbreviated time, as they work hard and come prepared to present with their originality and creativity.

(f) *In-class grouping*: This type of grouping is seen in elementary schools where teachers group children within class for working, reading etc., which could be called as peer grouping. Those with higher ability guide and help others—the peers, in the class.

(ii) Acceleration

Acceleration is another method of teaching the gifted. Acceleration means short promotion to another higher class or skipping over a class. There are various approaches which are commonly followed in the process of accelerations.

(a) *Formal*: The method of formal acceleration is skipping credit by examination and short-term promotion, to the next class.

(b) *The contract plan*: This method of acceleration provides for extra work for obtaining more credits than required thus be promoted to the next standard.

(c) *Early entrance*: In this type of acceleration, the homogeneity of mental age is favoured than homogeneity of chronological age and are admitted in schools and colleges irrespective of their chronological age.

(d) *Variation in academic load*: As gifted children are capable of doing more work they assigned extra academic load according to their interests and capability so that they do not feel bored in normal classroom situation.

(e) *Reduction in class time*: This approach basically emphasizes that gifted students attend regular classes but are excused on certain days to pursue some enriching activities according to their interests skipping routine work as average children do.

(iii) Enrichment

A resourceful teacher could enrich the existing curriculum in the following ways: Enrichment in regular class (increase in breadth of the activities for gifted children) and enrichment in depth, with high level thinking curriculum wherein importance is given to precision and intensive work. The following are some common approaches of enrichment programme.

(a) *Special assignments*: Gifted children are given special assignments which need more in-depth study of the topics.

(b) *Projects*: Projects may be of two types—individual and group. Individual project is often scientific investigation, the creative writing or social research. In group projects more than 2 or 3 children could participate and according to the ability of the individual child each one could contribute to complete the project.

(c) *Free choice activity:* Gifted children are allowed to choose activity of their interest from out of school subjects curriculum but these activities are not evaluated for scores and they do not get extra scores or credits for this.

(d) *Monitor and demonstrator*: Here, the intellectually superior children are made to be as helpers—to help the less able children with reading, writing and arithmetic.

(e) *Supervised correspondence study*: Extra study materials be provided to the gifted children to study on their own, it need not be only in the school or college. They could do it even at home, and earn two degrees or diplomas. This approach is used in higher secondary and above classes.

(f) *Provision for more materials*: Gifted children be provided with good books and laboratory equipments, so that they are encouraged to read more and do more experiments on their own.

(g) *Extra depth assignments*: Extra and special assignments are selected carefully by teachers to help the gifted to advance their knowledge of the subject.

(h) *Summer school*: Summer schools may be organised for different subjects for enriching the knowledge of gifted students, so that their leisure time could fruitfully be used and they also learn something according to their choice.

B. Teaching strategies for Gifted Children

Some of the best teaching strategies besides what have been already discussed, which can be used by the teachers for the maximum development of the potentialities of gifted children, are being discussed in the following pages.

***1. Self-Awareness Activities*:** Education of self-awareness is of very high importance for gifted children to enable them to utilize their potential and to be aware of their own talents. Two important self-awareness activities which can be of great importance in inculcating the quality of initiative, expression, independent decision making in gifted children are, Boundary Breaking activities and the other is the Encounter Lessons.

(a) Boundary Breaking Activities

Children are grouped into small groups with maximum of 20 and sit together. The leader begins a question and proceeds around the circle with each child responding intuitively. The leader is expected to be interested in listening as well as accepting. Some boundary-breaking questions are given below, as example:

(1) If you could be a plant, which would you choose?
(2) What is your favourite time of the day?
(3) Think of proud, and what do you recall?

The questions are arranged from simple to complex and asked. This activity is particularly good for the gifted because it demonstrates to them that they are different at the same time are also alike in many ways. Original thinking and creativity of children could be promoted. They can become 'Think Tanks'.

(b) Encounter Lessons

The University of Florida developed the technique of encounter lessons, which includes a number of activities that can be used for any age group just like boundary-breaking questions. These are short lessons of 15 to 20 minutes involving a small group of 8 to 10 members. They are active in learning lessons in which the one is truly to encounter others and their ideas. An example of encounter lesson prepared by Phyllis Strums, a teacher of the gifted is given:

Chairs Fantasy: Chairs fantasy is another game or activity which is used to foster creativity to identify with something and become that something and behave or act like that something.

Setting the Stage: Imagine that you are all chairs arranged around a dining table.

***Leading questions*:**

1. What is your position at the table?
2. What famous person would you like to sit upon you?
3. How would you feel if a 300 pound man sit upon you?
4. Whom would you like not to sit on you?

Evaluation Question

After the game or activity is over the teacher may further the following questions:

(1) Study and write about various styles of furniture and their history.
(2) Design a chair seat.
(3) Which type of arrangement you would prefer in your dining hall?

Encounter lessons create interest and motivate students to use their imagination and creativity.

***2. Independent Study*:** One of the important and promising areas for developing curriculum for the gifted is independent study because it builds upon the childs desire for self-initiated learning. The child here, thinks and initiates projects on his/her own.

3. Simulation: Gifted children are quite competitive and in simulation games, the students demonstrate critical, creative and logical thinking. In these games the children imagine act and interact. This promotes abstract thinking of children as they imagine of something or some situation and act.

Problems of Gifted Children

Gifted children many times face problems at home and school as they are different from average children. They also face problems to both parents and teachers if they are not properly understood by parents and teachers. Some problems are listed below:

Problems at Home

Gifted child sometimes appear as a 'fish out of water' at home. A child with abilities and interests quite outside the experience of his/her parents may feel dejected. These unusual interests may create problems for the gifted child, as others do not understand that these children possess extra, special activities.

Many times the parents find it difficult to answer to the questions of the gifted—which makes him/her feel frustrated. When parents fail to identify the giftedness in their children, they fail to provide suitable environment for his/her enrichment. So, there is possibility of these children becoming truant and run away from home to find a suitable environment which my make the child a problem child.

Problems in School

Gifted children in the school also face problems, the teacher as well as are listed below:

(1) The curriculum provided in traditional schools only suit the average child.
(2) The learning programme are not sufficiently challenging to the gifted.
(3) A gifted child tends to become bored and may opt out of such a situation by engaging in pursuit of his/her making which sometimes distrupts the class and antagonize the teacher-pupil relationship.
(4) The gifted child often pursues one interest so intensively that his work in other areas is neglected or not taken care of.

(5) Lack of sufficiently perceptive and resourceful teachers to recognize the abilities' and needs of gifted children.

Helping the Gifted

In addition to identifying and helping the gifted students we should also counsel them to make them adjust to the environment at home and school. Otherwise they will become outfit in the world and all their taken will be wasted. Promoting Moral courage, compassion, reflective judgement, responsibility commitment to goals, sense of wonder, ethical behaviour, creativity, autonomy, sense of self-efficacy, self-capitalization, contribution and commitment to society, global awareness, devotion to high ideas, high of moral development, advanced emotional development and wisdom should form part of guidance and counselling of the gifted children. Sometimes they feel they are not normal. Those who do not understand them properly also term them as abnormal.

Parents, teachers and the peer groups could identify many more ways of counselling gifted depending on the needs of the family and the values of society to be inculcated among the gifted children so that their abilities are not wasted, fully utilized to build a nation with intellectuals—creative writers, inventors, scientists, artists, religious leaders etc.

Review Questions

1. Define giftedness. Enumerate the various characteristics of gifted children.
2. Explain the various methods you will adopt to identify gifted children.
3. What are the problems faced by gifted children? How to overcome these?
4. Explain various intelligence tests for identifying giftedness.
5. Are you in favour of 'ability grouping'?. If so, how will you arrange for such grouping in your class?

6. What are the advantages and disadvantages of 'acceleration' in schools?
7. Briefly explain 'Enrichment classes for gifted children'.
8. Main streaming is considered to be the most appropriate method of educating gifted children. Discuss.
9. Integrated or inclusive education will be the solution to manage gifted children. Substantiate.
10. Bring out the relationship between 'Intelligent Quotient' and giftedness.

6

Learning Disabilities

If you enter any classroom in a high school, you will find two to three learning-disabled children. The number of such children is higher in those schools, which are situated in poverty-stricken surroundings and culturally disadvantaged areas of the country. The 'learning-disabled' are a group of children of normal intelligence who fail to learn because of neurogenetic learning disabilities. These children have been variously categorised as minimally brain-damaged, chronic brain syndromes, and minimal brain disfunction or psycho-neurological learning disabilities. This package tries to enrich your knowledge more on:

— The meaning of learning disabilities,
— The causes of learning disabilities,
— Characteristics of learning disabled,
— Identifying the learning disabled, and
— The educational provisions for disabled.

On completion of this package, you will be able to:

(1) Define 'Learning Disability',
(2) Enumerate the characteristics of learning disabled,
(3) Identify the causes of learning disability,
(4) Explain the methods of identifying learning disabled,
(5) List the types of learning disabilities,
(6) Describe the educational provisions for learning disabled.

Gopi in the third standard is not able to identify letters and finds if difficult to read like his follow classmates. He does not concentrate much in the class also. He also finds it difficult to write letters in the right form. Vasu in the fifth standard finds it difficult to recognize the numbers and very poor in calculation or mathematical functioning. Even the repeated efforts both by the teacher and these children fail in achieving the goal of reading, writing and calculating or mathematical operations.

Teacher reports that these children are hyperactive do not sit in one place and pay their attention in listening to their teachers. When they were referred to psychologist they diagnosed the problem of these children as the children with learning difficulties and advised for counselling and special attention by the teachers.

These are two case studies. But teachers find many more children like this in the classrooms and they find it difficult to handle them. More numbers of such children are to be counselled and guided. Let us see in the following package as to how the children with learning difficulties are to be identified and guided so that these children also fall in line with their counterparts in the classroom.

The term 'Learning Disability (LD) derives its meaning from the etiological concept of 'brain damaged', neural impairment, and its subsequent change to behavioural syndromes, popularly known as strauss-syndrome. These were later on known as children with learning disabilities characterised by hyper activity, distractibility, disinhibition and perseverance.

Learning disability is a disorder where the child has difficulty in learning or assimilating information to understand the world around them. There may be many causes for learning difficulty—Neurological deficit leading to abnormal functioning of brain, or maturational delay, foetal development, genetics, biochemical factors and medical factors such as prolonged hospitalization or even recurrent ear infection. Children with learning difficulties have minimal brain dysfunction, brain damaged, central process dysfunction and language delayed.

Here are few definitions of learning difficulties. According to Kirk (1962): "A learning disability refers to a retardation, disorder or delayed development in one or more of the processes of speech, language, reading, spelling, writing or arithmetic resulting from a possible cerebral dysfunction and/or emotional or behavioural disturbance and not from mental retardation, sensory deprivation or cultural or instructional factors".

According to **Learning Disabilities Act of 1969,** formed in 1977 Federal Register, "Specific Learning Disability means a disorder in one or more of the basic psychological processes involved in understanding or using language, spoken or written which may manifest itself in an imperfect ability to listen, think, speak, read, write, spell or to do mathematical education."

The Association for Children with Learning Disabilities (1967), define Learning disability as: "A child with learning disabilities is one with adequate mental ability, sensory processes and emotional stability who has a limited number of specific deficits in perceptual, integrative or expressive processes which severely impair learning efficiency. This includes children who have central nervous system dysfunction, which is expressed primarily in impaired learning efficiency.

According to **Johnson** and **Mykblebust**, "We refer to children as having psycho, neurological learning disability meaning that behaviour has been distrubed as a result of dysfunction of the brain and that the problem is one of altered process not of a generalised incapacity to learn."

National Joint Committee on Learning Disabilities (NJCLD) of America defines learning disabilities as follows:

"Learning disabilities is a genetic term that refers to a heterogenous group of disorders manifested by significant difficulties in the acquistion and use of listening, speaking, reading, writing, reasoning or mathematical abilities. These disorders are intrinsic to the individual and presumed to be due to central nervous system dysfunction, and may appear across the life span. Although learning difficulties may occur concomitantly with other handicapping conditions (for example sensory impairment, mental retardation, serious emotional disturbance) or with environmental influences (such as cultural differences, insufficient or inappropriate instruction) they are not the direct result of those conditions or influences.

According to **IDEA,** "Specific learning disability means a disorder in and/or more of the basic psychological processes involved in understanding or in using language, spoken or written which may manifest itself in an imperfect ability to listen, think, speak, read, write or do mathematical calculations. The term includes such conditions as perceptual handicaps, brain injury, minimal brain dysfunction, dyslexia and developmental abatia", (US Department of Education, 1992 a).

Symptoms of Learning Difficulties

Children with learning difficulties are either average or above average in their intelligent and academic achievement as they are poor in processing information which is essential for scholastic achievement. LD disturbs child's ability to read, write or mathematical computation leading to Dyslexia-difficulty with reading, Dysgraphia-difficulty in writing and Dyscalculia-difficulty in computing.

Types of Learning Difficulties

(1) Problems in Reading-Dyslexia: Children with severe reading problems are called dyslexic. Difficulties in this functioning may be due to visual, hearing or motor handicap, mental retardation or emotional disturbance or poor economic status.

(2) Difficulty in Writing-Disgraphia: This occurs due to dysfunction of central nervous system. They are severely impaired to write.

(3) Difficulty to Learn Mathematics-Dyscalculia: Children who have dyscalculia are severely impaired to calculate or have difficulty in mathematical functioning, due to dysfunction of central nervous system.

(4) Behaviour problems—either Hyperactive or Impulsive, Hyper active behaviour indicates impaired ability to sit in a place and concentrate for a long time. Children with impulsive behaviour cannot control their own behaviour.

These behaviours can occur due to Traumatic Brain Injury. Brain injury could also result in life long disabilities.

Alteration Deficit Disorder, also called Attention Deficit Hyperactivity Disorder (ADHD) is found among 3 to 5 per cent of school children. Owing to the lack of attention and hyper activeness these children's performance in academic activities is poor. They are poor achievers.

Characteristics of Children with Learning Disability

Learning Disability is primarily described as a deficit in academic achievement (reading, writing and arithmetic) or language (written language, listening, or oral language).

Clements (1966) identified the following ten characteristics of learning disabled children:

(1) Hyperactivity
(2) Perceptual motor impairments
(3) Disorders of attention
(4) Central co-ordination deficits
(5) Impulsivity
(6) Disorders of memory and thinking
(7) Specific learning disabilities (Reading, spelling, writing and arithmetic)
(8) Disorders of speech and hearing
(9) Equivocal neurological signs and electro-encephalographic irregularities.

Physical Signs of Learning Disabled

The following symptoms/signs are exhibited by children with Learning Difficulties.

(1) Mild tremor, mild aneroid movements
(2) Hyper reflex
(3) Excessive clumsiness
(4) Monocular vision

(5) Right-left confusion (impaired spatial concept)
(6) Impaired Perception
(7) Immature Articulation
(8) Hyper kinetic behaviour with distractibility.
Short attention span, irritability.

Classroom Behaviour

When you observe the children with Learning Difficulties you will find them with the following behaviour pattern in the classrooms.

(1) Poor visual discrimination and poor memory for words,
(2) Poor auditory memory for words or for individually sound in words,
(3) Persistent reversal of words in writing and speech,
(4) Poor recall for reproduction of simple geometric forms,
(5) Poor memory for auditory or visual experiences,
(6) Weakly established handedness,
(7) Clumsiness and poor hand control,
(8) Immature articulation, and
(9) Hyperactivity.

Group Characteristics

Children with learning disabilities are of various types and every individual has his/her own characteristics. But invariably they are low achievers in the school. Here it is not possible to describe the characteristics of individual child suffering from a specific learning disability but here, the group characteristics of children with learning disabilities are given:

— The learning and academic achievement of learning disabled children is of a very uneven pattern though they have average or above average intellectual potential, but due to damage to the specific area of brain their academic progress is not normal.

— Learning-disabled children look like other normal children and constitute 10 to 20 per cent of the total population of school going children.

— Most of the learning disabled children are boys but the reasons of high percentage of male children among disabled have not yet been known.

— A good percentage of learning disabled suffer from neurological defects.

— Learning disabled show gradual decrease in school/ classroom activities.

— Poor eye-hand co-ordination, right-left discrimination is common among children with learning disabilities.

— Defects in one or more sensory modalities could be observed.

— Perceptual defects are also found, among the children with learning disabilities.

— The social competence of children with learning disabilities is very poor. They find it difficult to use socially acceptable behaviour and misinterpret the social cues and behave inappropriately.

Specific Learning Difficulties

Reading (Dyslexia): Those who have disability in reading or dyslexia exhibit error in word recognition (omissions in sections, substitutions, reversals), errors in comprehension such as difficulty in recalling or deserving basic facts, sequence or theme, and other behaviours such as losing their place while reading or reading in a choppy and halting manner.

Writing (Dysgraphia): Difficulties in writing occurs in handwriting, spelling, productivity, text structure, sentence structure, lexicon and composition. Usually difficulties in language learning occur both in reading and writing. There is deficiency in phonological awareness also associated with this, which means those who have difficulty in learning language also have the difficulty in recognising sound segments in spoken word, as they do not have the ability to understand letter sound correspondence.

Mathematics (Dyscalculia): Poor performance in mathematics or computation is associated with the following:

(1) *Visual Perception*—i.e. difficulties in differentiating numbers, and special problems in copying shapes.
(2) *Memory*—have difficulty in recalling mathematical facts.
(3) *Motor Functions*—difficulties in writing numbers legibly or in small spaces.
(4) *Language*—difficulties in relating mathematic terms to real situation or in using mathematic vocabulary.
(5) *Abstract reasoning* is difficulty in solving problems and making comparisons.

Memory: We see students having difficulties in remembering what they learn, which also affects their performance in language and mathematics. This may be of (1) Poor, short-term memory relating to problems in rehearsal, organization, elaborative processing and phonological coding; (2) Long-term memory for tasks that require semantic processing; and (3) Working and executive memory functions for timely and organized ways of searching for information.

Meta cognition: Meta cognition means how one thinks and monitors one's thinking. People with learning difficulties have deficits in knowing strategies for acquiring, storing and processing information, understanding when, where and why these strategies are important in selecting and monitoring the use of these strategies wisely and reflectively.

Causes of Learning Disabilities

Causes of learning disabilities are many and no single factor can attribute as the only cause of learning disability.

The causes are classified as prenatal causes, perinatal causes, postnatal causes and Genetic/Hereditary influences.

Prenatal causes

The use of alcohol, smoking and other drugs such as cocaine result in learning difficulties in children. If mother is exposed, which causes malfornation of the developing brain and central nervous system. Sometimes if there is over exposure it will result in mental retardation also.

Perinatal causes

Traumas occur during birth process. This includes prolonged labour, anoxia, prematurity, or injury while using forceps.

Postnatal causes

High fever, encephalitis, meningitis, stroke, and head trauma are some of the causes for learning difficulties.

Genetic/Hereditary influences on learning difficulties are not yet properly identified, though few say that if the relatives have learning difficulties the child may acquire the same. But not yet confirmed as a definite reason for learning difficulties. Similarly, chromosomal abnormalities have also been cited as a cause of learning difficulties that also to be researched further.

The following are also identified as the causes of learning difficulties:

(1) *Maturational Lag*: Children, who fail to achieve maturation in physical and mental development, fail to achieve the anticipated standard required for learning to write, read, spell and speak. They are not brain injured. Their physical and intellectual development and maturity is not at the speed of normal children.

(2) *Neurological Disorganisation*: Some psychologists attribute many problems of learning and teaching disabled children to include neurological organization. This incomplete organization of the process of becoming organized due to brain injury prevents the child's central nervous system from becoming fully organized.

(3) *Educational Deficiency*: Poor teaching, poor attendance, poor curriculum, poor material, poor attitude, emotional blocks due to poor self-concept rather lack of confidence, interest in social affiliation, achievement, motivation, low

level of aspiration, family disorganization, lack of study skills, poor physical condition, lack of basic skills etc. due to brain injury prevents a child's central nervous system from becoming fully organized.

(4) *Neurological Syndrome*: A significant relationship is found between allergic reaction and hyper activity and learning disabilities.

(5) *Malnutrition and Vitamin Deficiency*: Lack of essential micro vitamins also causes learning disabilities.

(6) *Central Processing Dysfunction*: A Learning disability is also described as a problem involving deviation in the ability to process information. There is defect in the central processing of information involving disorder in receptacle analysis, synthesis and symbolic use. Children suffering from such problems may or may not have brain injury.

(7) *Minimal Brain Dysfunction*: Some physicians and educators attribute minimal brain damage as cause of learning disability.

Identification of Learning Disabled Children

Identification of Learning Disabled children involves the selection and application of diagnostic tests developed independently on each educational contents/subjects.

Hallahan and Kaufman (1978) identified five different types of tests that can be used as diagnostic measures for the identification and assessment of children with different kinds of learning disabilities.

(i) Norm Referenced Tests (NRT)

The Norm Referenced Tests make provision for the relative comparison of a child's score with another child of his age who has taken the same test. This comparison makes provisions for assessing the relative educational standing of children of the same age thereby revealing their educational deficits.

(ii) Process Tests (PT)

Process tests are ability tests indicating the level of mastery in a certain area of the educational subject. The process tests are designed with the assumption that the child encounters certain difficulties in processing certain concepts within the ability which has been designed to be measured by the educationists.

(iii) Informal Reading Inventories (IRI)

Reading abilities constitute a significant aspect of learning disabilities and stand as a consequential cause of educational deficits. Informal reading inventories developed by teachers by making use of a series of progressively more difficult sentences and paragraphs that the child is allowed to read aloud, can be used to identify the reading disabled children. Specific reading skills that require remediation can be identified and developed in the form of reading skill tests.

(iv) Criterion Referenced Tests (CRT)

The Criterion Referenced Test is designed to measure the score of the child in comparison to a predetermined criterion or mastery level. This test makes provision for comparison of the child's score under reference with a predetermined criterion score that has predictive significance. These tests are often developed by classroom teachers and make provision for direct measurement of the educational deficits of learning disabled. It is more or like Scholastic Achievement Test.

(v) Direct Daily Measuring Device (DDMD)

The school can make provisions for the systematic and regular recording of each child's performance on various specific skills of the teaching-learning process. Constant reinforcement and the feedback system employed by each teacher in his/her own subject can significantly help the children in improving their learning deficiencies. However, the success of the direct daily measurement system depends upon the honesty of purpose in teaching-learning process of the teachers.

Types of Learning Disabilities

***Ability Level*:** According to the intelleclual ability of children it is classified as children with:

(1) Average Intelligence,
(2) Near Average Intelligence, and
(3) Above Average Academic Ability.

***Activity Level*:** According to activity level, children are classified as:

(1) Hyperactive: The child is constantly engaged in motor activity, restlessness, tapping of finger or foot, jumping out of seat or skipping from task to task.
(2) Hyporactive: The opposite of hyperactivity—Fails to react or seems to do everything in slow motion.

Attention Problems

Short attention span: The child is unable to concentrate on anything for a longer period. There will be quick and frequent shifts in attention.

Preservation

Attention becomes fixed upon a single task, which is repeated over and over. It may be a motor activity or verbal topic.

Motor Problems

Lack of motor co-ordination and Poor tactile-kinesthetic are caused due to motor problem.

Visual Perceptual Problems

Discrimination: Unable to discriminate between two stimuli.

Visual figure ground: Unable to see foreground against a background.

Visual closure: Cannot fill in missing parts or portion when only part of an object is seen.

Visual memory: The child experiences difficulty in remembering images.

Auditory Perceptual Problems

Auditory discrimination: Unable to distinguish sounds.

Auditory comprehension: Fails to get meaning from the spoken word.

Auditory figure-ground: Unable to attend to important auditory stimuli.

Auditory closure: Cannot fill in the missing sound when only the part is heard.

Auditory memory: Experiences difficulty in remembering auditory stimuli or sound.

Work Habits

Poor organization confuses direction or rushes through work carelessly.

Social, Emotional and Behavioural Problems

Impulsive: Fails to stop to think the consequence of behaviour.

Explosive: Displays rage action or throws tantrum when crossed.

Social competence: Often below average. They adjust to change more slowly than others. Moods of such children vary often.

Orientation Problems

(1) Spatial organization: Poorly developed concept of space, distorted body image of left and right.
(2) Temporal concept: Experiences difficulty, in regard to time.

Educational Provisions for the Learning Disabled

Special Educational Programmes

As the learning disabled are with specific disabilities, this disability needs to be diagnosed first of all by employing specific goal-directed techniques. Then, as per the amount and nature of the learning disabilities, the special educational remedial measures can be provided to him with care and caution, without disturbing his emotional state.

School Services

The educational deficits of the learning disabled may be met by effective school services:

(i) The school psychologists, teachers, guidance workers, social workers, counsellors and parents as well as principals can render effective services to the learning disabled by playing their specific roles.
(ii) Help the children with learning difficulties to adopt to the environment and with the peer group.
(iii) Help them learn rather than teaching, by giving individual attention.
(iv) Provide opportunity to learn in small group and encourage peer tutoring.
(v) Giving small assignment to have a sense of completion and achievements.
(vi) Individualized, positive reinforcement including seating arrangement tc motivate learning.

(vii) Provision of regular classroom, specialized teachers, use instructional aids and computer and resource rooms will ensure special training for these children.

(viii) Specially trained teachers should be appointed to train these children. The teacher should be technically trained and socially desirable traits like positive self-concepts, a desire to have social status and prestige and a positive attitude to life can be considered as desirable behavioural requirements of these special teachers.

Review Questions

1. Define 'Learning Disability'.
2. How will you identify the learning disabled?
3. What are the factors that lead to learning disability?
4. Enumerate the common characteristics of learning disabled.
5. Analyze the causes of learning disabilities.
6. How will you educate the learning disabled?
7. What is the role of teachers in identifying children with Learning Disability?

7

Autism

We observe some children are very active in all the dimensions of human behaviour. They communicate well social, highly imaginative; and some are poor in their communication, they avoid looking at other's eyes while speaking, they don't mingle or interact with others freely and are not imaginative. What makes these differences? The first categories of people are normal and the second categories are called Autistics. Let us now analyse the behaviour pattern of a child before we further proceed with this lesson.

Venu is a 3-year-old boy and he is now in the pre-primary class. He is very active; runs here and there without concentrating on any task in the school. He goes on repeating the same act and same words/sentence even when he plays with peer group. He wants to stick on to the same types of activities and does not want to have change in the environment, as he likes to involve only in stereotype of activities.

Ragu is a five-year old boy. He wants to avoid the company of his parents and even does not like to hold their hands when they go out for a walk. He avoids being in the company of anyone. He likes to be alone. His teacher tries to take him to the group of other children; but fails in her attempt, as Ragu does not want to see even her eyes. When he is alone he hurts himself and suffers the pain and bleeding.

Why do these children behave like this? Don't we observe many more children both at home and school? How do other children react to these types of behaviours and children? What will be their future? How will they adjust with others at home and the community?

We shall discuss about this type of children and our responsibility towards them.

Objectives of the Lesson

On reading this lesson you should be able to:

- — Understand what is autism
- — Define autism
- — Identify the characteristics of autism
- — List the causes of autism
- — Identify the appropriate educational procedure for children with autism.

Autism has been defined by IDEA as:

"Autism means developmental disability significantly affecting verbal and non-verbal communication and sound interaction, generally evident before age 3, that adversely affects educational performance. Other characteristics are often associated with autism are engagement in repetitive activities and stereotyped movements, resistance to environmental changes or changes in daily routines and unusual responses to sensory experiences. The term does not apply if a child's educational performance is adversely affected primarily, because the child has a serious emotional disturbance. [34 C.F.R. Part 300, Sec.300-7 (e) (1).]

Autism is a biological disorder that generally lasts through out a person's life. It is a developmental disability as it starts before a child reaches 3 years when the development is rapid. This condition either delays the growth or causes developmental problems. Children with autism have problems in communication both verbal (spoken) and non-verbal (unspoken). Social interaction with other people both physical and verbal such as hugging or holding and having conversation with others, have receptive or routine stereotyped behaviours like repeating words or actions over and over or following a very specific ways of arranging their belongings. They have good role memory but don't have imagination. They prefer to be alone.

All the people with autism do not have the same type of symptoms, as it is a complex disorder, which affect people differently. Some children with autism may not like their parents holding their hands. They always want to come out of their parent's or others holding. Similarly, adults with autism avoid looking at others eyes and some may not know how to talk or never learn to talk. These behaviours make their life difficult and miserable and also make life of the people at home, other health care providers, their teachers and anyone who comes in contact with them. Some people injure themselves by head banging, biting or scratching. This may permanently injurious.

Those who are with mild symptoms of the disorder are called people with "Autism Spectrum Disorder (ASD)". It is a neurological disorder that presents people from understanding what they see, hear or sense. It also affects social interaction, reasoning and communications. It can also affect the functioning and development of the brain if it affects before the child is three years old.

Causes

No specific cause has been associated with autistic behaviours in children. It is a general one and connected with numerous their unrelated disorders, like schiyophrema (term used to describe characteristic behaviours like serious thought disturbances, withdrawal, inappropriate emotional response or lack of emotional response, hallucination and delusion), depression and learning difficulties. So ASD is not a single disease but a constellation of observable behaviours that appear to be uniquely related (Newsom & Recover, 1981).

Some say that ASD manifest due to genetic or biochemical variables. It is three times common among boys than in girls. It is also found to be positively correlated with presence of fragile and syndrome [Fisch, *et al.* 1986]. It is also suggested that ASD is also due to lack of environmental stimulation during early childhood years.

Biomedical causes like abnormality in brain development or brain damage also is responsible for autism. Abnormalities are found in the area of cerebellum and in the cerebral cortex.

Educational Procedures

Educational procedures are to be planned on the basis of the type of behaviours exhibited by them so that learning becomes easier for them. A proper diagnosis and analysis of the behaviour should determine the curriculum and the methodology to be followed to educate these children. Some children have higher mental ability and some are retarded with learning difficulties, some children may have normal or average IQ.

Individualization of education-curriculum and instruction will help autistic children learn better whether at school or at home. Education for these children should promote life skills for integrated community living, prepare them for some vocations and provide functional academics, which include providing language and communication skills. A positive behaviour support should be provided. Multiple approaches should be adapted for teaching the Autistic children. The behaviour intervention programme should help them increase their self-confidence and image and increase their dignity. Special programme like music, drawing, dancing, games etc., could be introduced. Now computer assisted learning (CAL) materials are also available for Autistic children as it caters to the individual requirement, interest and activities.

Methodology

Inclusive and collaboration in educating the children with autism should be encouraged. There should be active parental involvement in the development and implementation of the programme. Proper technical support should be given to the faculty members and the family members. Programme planned should integrate and match children's learning style and interests. Peer group should be encouraged to have a positive approach and be involved in teaching the autistic children. Parents should be encouraged to observe their children at school, i.e., school based observations. Home-based parent education by the faculty members twice or three times a week by visiting their homes and educating the parents on how to promote communication skills, appropriate play activities to be introduced will help parents to take care of autistic children, at home more efficiency.

Parent support group established in the school should meet once a month and discuss about issues relating to care and education of their children. Parent teacher liaison should help as to how the crisis management could take place at home; crisis management group could help the parents if they need any special assistance.

Besides these the following strategies could also be adopted to mainstream these children, with autism.

(1) Home-based programming;
(2) Peer group to teach social skills;
(3) Preparing families for incidental teaching and advocacy;
(4) Increasing the interaction with significant people in the society; and
(5) Intensive, individualised instruction approximately forty hours a week.

Childcare services for the children with autism should aim at providing equitable, affordable, flexible and high quality childcare and to ensure the growth in the child care sector is sustainable. Best care of their children should become national priority.

Review Questions

1. Who is an autistic child?
2. Define autism.
3. Identify a child with autism and list its characteristics.
4. What procedures are to be followed to educate children with autism?
5. How will you educate the parents of autism?
6. Suggest other strategies to be followed to mainstream the autistic children.

8

The Creative Child

The almighty God, the creator of the universe, is the supreme mind who possesses the finest creative abilities. Everyone of us, created by that supreme power is a unique creation; but one does not possess the same creative ability as his peers or siblings. Good education, proper care and provision of opportunities for creative expression inspire, stimulate and sharpen the creative mind.

Creativity is inherent among all creatures and linked with giftedness. A few people have greater creative talents and had contributed to advancement in their specialized fields, like Mahatma Gandhi, Abraham Lincoln, Homi Bhabha, Newton, Einstein Shakespeare and many more. Thus creativity is related to any field of individual interest. Creativity does exist in persons in varying quantity and every person has his field of peculiarities in varying degrees of complexity.

Defining Creativity

The term 'creativity' or 'creative process' has been defined in many ways. Some of these definifions are as follows:

Spearman, C. (1931): Creativity is the power of the human mind to create new contents by transforming relations and thereby generating new correlates.

Stagger and Karwoski (1956): Creativity implies the production of a 'totally' or 'partially' novel identity.

Drevdahl (1956): Creativity is the capacity of a person to produce compositions, products or ideas which are essentially new or novel and previously unknown to the producer.

Dehaan and Havinghurst (1961): Creativity of the children is the quality which leads to the production of something new and desirable. The new product may be new to society or new to the individual, who creates it.

Guilford (1959): Creative children have a more general trait that includes not only originality, but flexibility, fluency, motivational and temperamental traits as well.

Gardner (1988): Creativity is the capacity to regularly solve problems or fashion new products in one or more domains of activity.

By incorporating all these viewpoints, creativity can be described as the capacity or ability of an individual to create, discover, or produce a new or novel idea or object, including the rearrangement or reshaping of what is already known to him which proves to be a unique personal experience. It is said that the correlation between intelligence and creativity is weak for people with IQ scores over 100.110. (Barron), Harrington, (1982). Few creative activities need more intelligent like in science discovery than in literature, paintings and sculptors.

Characteristics of Creative Person

Creative children can be recognised because of their characteristics such as:

(1) Courageous and adventurous.
(2) Have a controlled imagination which provides guidance to any achievement.
(3) Has intellectual freedom. He/she is independent in thinking and judgement.
(4) He/she has patience to tolerate oppositions.
(5) He/she becomes absorbed and preoccupied in what he/she is doing.
(6) He/she provides diverse responses which invite social attention. He/she has the ability to participate in various fields of activity.
(7) He/she is visionary and optimistic.

(8) He/she is willing to take risks.
(9) He/she has intellectual self-confidence.
(10) He/she is generally labelled as introvert.
(11) Though such children have the creative ability, intelligence. It is not necessary that they should get the highest marks in intelligence tests.
(12) They would like to be independent, curious, spontaneous alert, flexible, sensitive, initiative and insightful.
(13) Intrinsically motivated, as the activity is inheritantly compelling, enjoyable and satisfying.
(14) Have less extrinsic motivation for external rewards.
(15) Creative children are found to be less social, more sensitive and guided by their inner feelings.
(16) They have a healthy mind.
(17) The creative children are more mature than their age and always introduce novelty in the atmosphere.
(18) They are honest, faithful and have the ability to talk to others with originality.

Identification of Creative Potential

In the preceding pages we discussed few of the characteristics of creative children. Identifying a creative child is a multi-dimensional approach involving the use of testing devices like creative tests and non-testing devices like observation, interview, rating scale, personality inventory, situational tests, interest inventories, attitude scales, aptitude tests, value schedules and projective techniques etc.

Creativity Tests

Creativity tests may be used in identification of the creatives in the same way as intelligence. Some of these are enumerated below:

Tests standardized abroad

(1) Minnesota tests of creative thinking.
(2) Guilford's divergent thinking instruments.

(3) Remote association tests.
(4) Torrance tests of creative thinking.

Tests standardized in India

(1) Bager Mehdi's tests of creative thinking.
(2) Passi's tests of creativity.
(3) Sharma's divergent production abilities.
(4) Saxena's tests of creativity.

Given below are some verbal and non-verbal activities given in those creative tests:

(a) **Figure/Picture Completion test**: In this sub-test, there are some incomplete figures and the subjects are asked to complete those figures by adding her/his dimensions or lines for providing new ideas. For Example: Draw a Man Test, with incomplete figure of a man.
(b) **Figural Construction test**: In this test, the subject is provided with a piece of coloured paper and the subject is asked to think of a figure of which the piece of paper may be a part.
(c) **Picture Construction test**: Here, there are two simple geometrical figures, viz., a semicircle and a rhombus. The subject has to construct and elaborate pictures using each figure as an integral part of the picture.

The verbal forms of creative tests involve the use of language. Some of the verbal items in creative tests are:

(a) **Asking type:** In this activity, the subject is asked to reveal her/his ability to perceive all things which are not normally perceived by others. Pictures may be used for this purpose. In these activities the subject is asked to fill in the gaps in her/his knowledge.
(b) **Product-improvement type**: In these activities, the subject is asked to suggest ways and means of improving a toy, a machine or some other such product to make it as interesting and as useful as possible.

(c) **Unusual Uses type or Divergent uses type**: These devices are meant to test the subject's divergent thinking about the number of ways in which a product may be used. Here the subject has to enumerate as many unusual uses as she/he thinks she/he can. For example, 'in how many unusual ways can a knife/brick be used?

(d) **Unusual question type:** In these activities, the subject is asked to suggest unusual questions about a picture/scene.

(e) **Just suppose type**: In these activities the subject is required to predict the outcomes of unusual situation. For example, what would have happened had you been provided with another set of eyes at the back of your head?

Problems of Creativity

When environmental conditions foster the development of mental rigidity or convergent thinking, it will prevent the development of mental flexibility or divergent thinking. Equally serious is anything that encourages spending too much time on certain forms of creativity. For example, occasional daydreaming may lead to good personal and social adjustments. But excessive daydreaming is harmful. There are number of hazards to good adjustment in different areas of creativity:

*1. **Failure to stimulate creativity***: Even though the foundations for creativity are innate, like all innate potentials, its development must be stimulated. Any condition that obstructs the stimulation will prevent its development. Lack of stimulation may be due to ignorance on the part of parents and teachers.

*2. **Unfavourable social attitudes towards creativity***: Social factors often impede the development of creativity. These obstructive factors take two common forms:

(i) Unfavourable attitudes towards children who are creative; and

(ii) Lack of social rewards for creativity.

The children soon realise that the school encourages and rewards convergent thinking and not potentially creative divergent thinking. Obstructive social attitudes and lack of rewards not only discourage creativity but even worse, they lead to maladjustive behaviour by developing in the child an unfavourable self-concept.

***3. Unfavourable home conditions*:** Discouragement of exploration by children, regimentation of time, encouragement of family togetherness and little regard for personal interests and preferences, discouragement of fantasy, provision of highly structured play equipment, conservative parents, over protective parents and authoritarian discipline are the main constraints against a favourable environment for development of creativity.

***4. Unfavourable school conditions*:** Very large classes where regimentation is classicality, strong emphasis on memorization, discouragement of anything that does not original painting/original story telling, a highly organised schedule of class activities, strict, authoritarian discipline and the belief of teachers that creative children are hard to manage and their work is harder to grade than the conformers act as obstacles to stimulate the natural talents of creative children.

***5. Excessive daydreaming*:** Daydreaming is one of the most potentially dangerous form of creativity because it can so readily become habitual method of escaping from unpleasant realities. But this does not mean that all daydreaming is dangerous. Too little daydreaming is almost as hazardous to good adjustment as too much daydreaming.

Educating the Creative Children

Creativity, as a natural endowment needs stimulation and nourishment from parents and teachers. Most creative talent, unless it is given proper training, education and opportunities for expression is wasted. Proper stimulation and nurturing of the traits which help develop creativity, namely originality, flexibility, ideational fluency, divergent thinking, self-confidence, persistence, sensitiveness, ability to see relationship and make associations are essential for educating children with creativity. This may be achieved through the following practices, in the school environment.

1. Freedom to respond: Most often teachers and parents kill the creative spark by breeding conformity and passivity. Freedom to express and originality in thoughts has to be developed in children. We must also let them have their own way when they need a particular kind of novel expression of their ideas, without any inhibition.

2. Opportunity for ego involvement: Feeling that 'this is my creation,' 'I have solved it,' give much satisfaction to children. Actually, a child can be expected to put in determined efforts into creative activities only when his ego is involved, i.e. when he/she feels that a particular creative work is the outcome of her/his efforts. We should, therefore, provide opportunities to children to derive satisfaction from identifying themselves as the cause of a product or creator or a discoverer.

3. Removal of internal blocks to creativity: In order to prepare children for creative productivity, they must be helped to feel secure with their relationships with others, without worrying about the acceptability of their ideas. We generally come across comments like, 'I know what I mean, but I cannot write/speak before others'. The causes of such diffidence and inhibition should be removed and the children should be encouraged to speak and express themselves no matter how crude the subject is.

4. Providing appropriate opportunities and atmosphere for creative expression: A healthy atmosphere, favourable for creative thinking and expression is essential for the stimulation and nourishment of creativity in children. Co-curricular activities, celebration of festivals, social get-to-gathers, and even regular class-work can be arranged in such a way to stimulate and develop creative thinking in children.

5. Keeping fantasy alive: Fantasy is not only essential in helping children's mental growth and adjustment, it is also a vital ingredient in creativity. Every effort, therefore, has to be made to discourage the school and the home from communicating the belief to children that such flights of imagination are signs of immature thinking.

6. Developing healthy habits among children: Industriousness, persistence, self-reliance and self-confidence are some of the qualities that are helpful to creative output of children. Therefore, they should be helped to imbibe these qualities, from early childhood. Moreover, they should be encouraged to stand up against criticism of their creative expression. They should be made to feel that whatever they create is unique and freely express what they desire to express.

7. Using the creative resources of the community: Children should be made to visit the centres of art, scientific, and industrial creative work. This may stimulate and inspire them for creative work, Experts could be invited to interlay with children to kindle the spark of creativity in them.

8. Proper organization of the curriculum: Learning experiences in the form of curricular, extra and co-curricular activities should be so designed to foster creativity among children. For this purpose, the school curriculum should be organized on the basin of concepts rather than facts. The curriculum should reflect what is expected from the creative children in terms of fluency, flexibility, originality, divergent thinking, inventiveness discovery, description, elaboration etc.

9. Reform in the evaluation system: If creativity is to be nurtured, evaluation system has to be completely reformed at all levels. Now the emphasis is on memorization by rote, fixed and single rigid response, convergent thinking etc. which kill creativity of the children. This system should be discouraged and a proper evaluation system be adopted for encouraging complete and balanced experiences in developing the creative behaviours of children.

10. Techniques of fostering creativity: Some special techniques for fostering creativity have been suggested here:

(i) ***Brainstorming*:** Brainstorming is a strategy or technique for allowing a group of children to explore ideas without judgement or censure. In practice, the children may be asked to sit in a group for solving problem and attacking it without any inhibition, from many angles. The students are to be asked to suggest ideas as rapidly as possible. All ideas are encouraged and appreciated, therefore, no

criticism is allowed during the brainstorming session. They are not restricted to new ideas only but are also encouraged upon ideas put forward by fellow students. At the end of the session, the ideas received from all should be discussed in a free, frank and open environment and the most viable ideas are accepted for solution of the problem in hand.

(ii) ***Use of teaching models***: Some of the teaching models developed by educationists may prove quite beneficial in developing creativity among children. For example, Brenner's concept attainment model helps in developing creativity in children for the attainment of various concepts.

(iii) ***Use of games***: Gaming techniques, in a playful spirit, help the children in the development of creative traits. Both verbal and non-verbal stimulus materials are used in such techniques. For instance, in verbal transaction of ideas, children may be asked to name all the round things they think of, tell all the different ways a knife can be used, or complete an incomplete story.

In non-verbal transactions the children may be asked to build a cube, complete a picture and build or construct something or anything out of the materials given to them.

Review Questions

1. Define creativity. Identify the characteristics of a creative person.
2. How will you identify creativity with the help of standardised tests?
3. What are the hazards of creativity?
4. Give your suggestions to provide suitable education for the creative children.
5. What is the role of teachers and parents in fostering creativity?

9

Educational Backwardness

Wilson is a 15-year-old boy. He is studying in 8th standard. He is a repeater—he failed in many classes. He does not concentrate much on the class work, but indulges in anti-social activities. He smokes and sometimes plays truant also. The curriculum of the school seems to be too difficult for him, though his class fellows enjoy learning. His parents with the advice of the Head of the school approached a Counsellor. After many sittings with the boy Counsellor found that Wilson as a Backward child and needs not only counselling but also a conducive atmosphere at home.

In the case of Saji it is different. She exhibits extraordinary interest in her studies. Suddenly one fine morning she lost her parents in a disaster and she was brought to a home for the orphans. Though she had interest in her studies sudden loss of her parents and living in a different type of atmosphere in the orphanage made her lose interest in everything and she is not able to adjust to the new environment. She seeks individual attention that could not be given there in the institution where she is living. So she refuses to go to school and even if she is sent to school she absconds from there. A devoted teacher can narrate many more cases like these.

Some children cannot progress in their class with others in their age group. They do not show any interest in learning and do not like to take part even in curricular and co-curricular activities. They are of normal IQ and become educationally backward in their class due to their low academic achievement. This package gives you an overall idea on:

— Who are educationally backward?
— Causes of backwardness.
— Characteristics of backward children.
— Identification of backwardness.
— Educating the educationally backward.

On completion of this package, the reader will be able to

(1) Define 'educational backwardness'.
(2) List the causes of educational backwardness.
(3) Explain the tests and non-test techniques used for identifying educational backwardness.
(4) Enumerate the characteristics of backward children.
(5) Describe the educational provisions for backward children.

Backwardness is a relative concept, which can be used to express any low achievement or mental ability or progress in any field. This term is used for low-level achievement of education. This may be in one or two subjects. Backwardness is that specific psychological attribute which affects the total development of the personality of a child. The term 'backward children' and 'backwardness' has been defined in many ways.

Barton Hall (1947)

Backwardness, in general, is applied to cases where their educational attainment falls below the level of their natural abilities.

Schonell (1948)

Backward pupil is one who, compared with other pupils of the same chronological age, shows marked educational deficiency.

Burt (1950)

Backward child is one who in his normal school career is unable to do the work of the class which is done by a normal one of his age.

Causes of Backwardness

Many factors are responsible for children being backward. The causes are classified, as 'within' the child and the environmental causes.

1. Causes within the child

(i) Subnormal physical and physiological development

The educational achievement of a child mostly depends upon physical and physiological factors. Backward children are less competent than normal children due to their abnormal physical development.

Physical disabilities (or) inabilities like visual defects, audio defects, speech defects, physical abnormality, left-handedness etc. are the hindrances to the students' progress. The result is lack of proper adjustment in school, long absenteeism etc.

(ii) Mental Retardation and low general intelligent

This is a very serious factor. These children become backward due to congenital general mental ability or trauma in the brain. The intellectual retardness affects their achievements in the class also. If there is logical ability, thought power, imagination, observation and unity, the mental ability of a child cannot be promoted. So, they experience difficulty in doing their daily routine work and remain unsuccessful in life.

(iii) Faulty Emotional Development

Faulty emotional development is an individual case of backwardness in which he suffers from such complexes and emotions, which create obstacles in his progress according to his abilities. For example, superiority and inferiority complexes, negative attitude towards teachers and education, will be barriers in the achievements of such children.

2. Causes within the Environment or Environmental Causes

(i) Home Environment

The privileged rich and well-to-do families are able to provide the best amenities of life and good education to their children. Children belonging to poor families on the other hand, are left alone without proper education, are denied even the basic necessities of life and they are deprived of many things which they would like to have. Their health suffers as a result of malnutrition and unhygienic living conditions. This impairs their capacity for learning and they become backward.

In poor homes the children are often required to help in many household chores or to augment the family income. As a result, they devote less time to their studies. They also become tired of the household work and thus are unable to devote proper attention to their studies at home as well as at school.

Besides poverty, the intellectual inferiority and illiteracy of the parents also contribute towards sub-normal educational attainment of the children. Such parents have neither a positive attitude towards education nor the ability to guide and help the children in their studies.

The strained relationships and improper behaviour not only disturb the harmony at home, but also create many emotional and social problems. In the families where the parents are divorced or the child has a father or stepmother or where the parental attitudes are either too harsh or too indulgent or where there are unusual conflicts and quarrels, the child's psychological and social needs are not satisfied. In this kind of environment, the child neither feels secure nor gets enough love, affection and guidance from his parents and hence becomes educationally backward.

(ii) School Environment

Inappropriate school atmosphere, unfavourable and non-conducive environmental conditions also contribute to the problem of backwardness. The following factors operating in school may affect the educational attainment of the children:

(1) Defective, uninteresting and ineffective teaching.
(2) Lack of equipment, infrastructure facilities and provision for revision, experimental and creative work, co-curricular and extra-curricular activities.
(3) Defective curriculum and examination system.
(4) Lack of guidance and wrong choice of subjects by the children.
(5) Poor administration and indiscipline in the school.
(6) No regular checking of home assignment and lack of proper incentives and stimulation.
(7) Improper attitudes of the teacher and inter-personal relationships among the staff and students.

(iii) Influence of neighbourhood and other social agencies

The social environment of the child is not confined within the boundary walls of his home or the school. The neighbourhood where the child lives, the companions, peer group with whom he plays and the gang with whom he associates himself, the members of the society he comes in contact with, the press, radio, cinema, clubs, religious and social places that he visits, all contribute to the problem of educational backwardness. Any or all of these may colour his attitude towards life or study and also divert his attention to other socially undesirable activities in the place of studies and consequently causes scholastic backwardness or low achievement.

Identification of Backwardness

For the proper treatment and identification of these children, timely diagnosis is very much necessary. Standardized tests and mental ability tests are also used to identify them. A few tests and techniques in use are described here.

1. General Mental Ability or Intelligence Tests

From administration of standardized tests and the scores obtained the following inferences are drawn:

IQ Range	*Inference*
70 to 84	Dull mental ability (Backward equally in all subjects)
Below 70 IQ	Low mental ability (Unable to avail education)
More than 85	Normal mental ability (reasons of backwardness are not intelligence or dullness)

2. Standardized Achievement Tests

Standardized achievement tests are used to determine the real educational achievement in the class. These tests measure the acquired knowledge of the child in any special school subject. It can be identified whether the child is backward equally in all subjects or in anyone subject. Though the reason of backwardness can be known by the half yearly and annual marks of examination, a few standardized tests are also available for measuring their achievement in the school.

1. L.N. Dubey Hindi Achievement Test
2. Saroj Aurora Biology Achievement Test
3. S.N.L. Bhargava Physics Achievement Test
4. Vidyawathi Malaya, K.C. Malaya, L.N. Dubay Adult Education Achievement Tests
5. A.K. Singh and Para Sen Gupta-General Classroom achievement test for class 6th and 7th.

3. Diagnostic Test

Diagnostic tests have been developed to understand the typical weakness in a particular subject of the children who do not have low IQ. The main objective of this test is to find out the weaknesses in a particular subject of the children so that they can be given special attention and guidance on this subject. The total scores do not have any value in diagnostic scales but only part scores, which indicate a child's weaknesses and difficulties. For example, if a child cannot solve the sum of ratio, it does not mean that he has no ability of solving them but it may be due to weakness in solving problems of multiplication and division. It may be that one child faces difficulty in doing division and another faces in multiplication. This shortcoming can be pointed out easily by diagnostic tests.

4. Other Psychological Tests

Sometimes, the backwardness may be psychological too. For example, the maladjustment of the child at home and in school, social and emotional, lack of motivation and morale, ignorance about utility of education and special subjects, and negative attitude towards interest, mental conflicts, anxiety, tension may affect the child's achievement in the school subjects.

Different standardized psychological tests, interview, and discussions with parents and teachers etc., can provide information, which can help in developing techniques for diagnosing the causes for educational backwardness.

5. Knowledge of Various Situations and Behaviours

The child's socio-economicstatus, the academic status of the parents, attendance of child in class for the whole year, time of admission in school, frequent transfers from schools, school atmosphere, cognitive status of teachers, teaching and instructional aids used by teachers etc. are very helpful in identifying the external causes of child's educational backwardness. Besides these, various other situations like the child's behaviour in the class, at home, in the playground, library, as well as during classroom teaching can also provide reasonable information to identify the causes for backwardness. Anecdotes of the child's reactions in various situations are also helpful in diagnosing the casual factors of backwardness.

Characteristics of Backward Children

The following are being identified as the characteristics of backward children:

(1) The learning speed of these children is very slow.
(2) They develop an attitude of pessimism about life.
(3) They show the tendency to indulge in anti-social act.
(4) Various problems are manifested in their behaviour.
(5) They have relatively low-academic achievement as compared to their inherent abilities.
(6) They cannot derive benefit from the general school curriculum.
(7) They are unable to get education by general learning techniques.
(8) They are involved in mentally unhealthy and maladjusted behaviour.
(9) They have low IQ with a mean ranging from 40 to 90 or even below it.
(10) They exhibit ability to make steady progress like other normal children.
(11) They fail to develop higher mental thought process.

Education of the Backward Children

The problem of educational backwardness is a major problem for educationists. This leads to huge wastage of time and money. To remove their backwardness group efforts are required. The following educational provisions may be useful:

1. Special Educational Provisions

These children when taught in schools with the other educationally normal children are unable to cope with class work. These children cannot adjust in classrooms. Therefore, we should provide special treatment by using the following methods:

(i) *Special Classes*: The children who are educationally backward cannot be taught large in a class. They encounter or develop psychological problems due to continuous failure. They may not feel frustrated and will not be conscious of the problems of maladjustment if they are in a separate class. The teacher has to use improvised techniques and special learning materials by keeping in view their progress reports, intellectual status etc. for optimum reference as all children have an equal educational status in the special class.

(ii) *Special Schools*: Children who are educationally backward, with a low IQ should be taught in special schools because they are so different that they cannot be educated in a general class and by the same learning materials as used for teaching normal children. They require separate special schools.

(iii) *Specified Curriculum*: Generally, a curriculum is based on the requirements of average children. But the backward children fail to meet them adequately. So it is better to devise a curriculum according to their personal needs, interests and efficiency. Manual skill like handworks, woodwork, and bookbinding should be included in their curriculum.

(iv) *Teaching Methods*: The teaching methods for backward children have to be remodelled appropriately. They should be taught by dividing the subject matter into small units with the help of concrete objects and direct experiences. Drill and practice in the units taught is necessary. Use of audio-visual materials, learning by doing, projects and play-way methods are to be encouraged.

(v) *Special Teachers*: The teachers should be specially trained to teach children with educational backwardness and experienced. They should have knowledge of psychology and have insight and interest to know the special shortcomings and difficulties of these children. They should be trained to have enough patience to teach and take pains despite the continuous failure of children without getting irritated.

(vi) *Diversified Courses*: The absence of extra-curricular and co-curricular activities in schools creates boredom. Arrangement for games, field visits, entertainments, library etc. are required for them besides their texts and the prescribed syllabus. They should be given chances for acting, dancing, music, art and leadership training according to their individual differences and capacity. Training in creative arts, handicrafts should be encouraged.

(vii) N.C.C. safety rules, first aids etc. motivates the children, with educational backwardness, and they learn with interest.

(viii) *Timetable:* Backward children cannot concentrate for a long time. They are unable to progress as the normal children do. It is, therefore, imperative to make a separate timetable for them. It should be flexible with small periods and give importance to co- and extra-curricular activities.

(ix) *Examination System*: Psychological backwardness should be evaluated on the basis of a child's own achievements within her/his mental abilities of his/her own mental age and not chronological age. The teachers who teach them should set the question papers and test the backward children. The question paper should be more objective and easy language should be used. Only those questions with which they are familiar should be asked to promote the sense of achievement.

2. Checking Non-attendance and Truancy

Non-attendance or absentism and truancy are the external causes of backwardness. Sometimes, these children become backward, due to this negative attitude over a long time and they make false excuses for not attending classes and do not take any interest in the school activities. So one of the preventive as well as curative measures is to invite the attention and participation of parents in resolving the problems of absence from school and truancy.

3. Provision of Guidance Services

Sometimes children become unsuccessful due to improper guidance in selection of subjects and other activities in the schools. Guidance services in the proper way is essential to help the children choose various subjects according to their aptitude, interest, attitude and ability. If they are not guided properly it may lead to failure and frustration.

4. Controlling Negative Environment Factors

Unsocial, unhealthy environment, illiterate peers, negative values etc. around affect the backward child. Control of such factors is very much essential for prevention of backwardness.

5. Help from Experienced Educational Psychologists

The services of experienced educational psychologists can be very useful in educating children with psychological backwardness. They can mobilize, control and re-design those courses related to the child's backwardness, so that the child is not influenced by negative environmental factors.

Review Questions

1. Define 'educationally backward children'.
2. What are their characteristics?
3. Explain the factors leading to educational backwardness.
4. As a teacher, how will you diagnose educational backwardness of your children and what remedial measures do you suggest for their betterment?
5. How can the external environment be modified or controlled to suit the backward children?

10

Behavioural Disorders and Emotional Disturbances

Latha is a six-year-old girl. She refuses to sit in the class. She wants to be always walking around without sitting in one place and listening to the teacher. She just cannot play with any log or material for more than 10 minutes at a stretch. She attracts the attention of the teacher by throwing things around or by loathing another child. She finds it to adjust with her peer group. There are many children in the school from lower Pre-Primary to Higher Secondary. Each one with varied problems expressing through different ways.

Jeeva an orphan living in a hostel longs for the affection. She wants at least some one to care for her and speak nice words to her. She sees other children enjoying the weekends with their parents and other soloing. Jeeva then feels lonely. She runs away from the hostel forgetting the attention of the caretakers of the hostel. Is she a truant? Why does she run away from hostel? When she is brought back to the hostel by the police she is ill treated that aggravated the situation. She refuses to eat and do anything in the hostel. She does not want to listen to the hostel authority. She is then taken to a remand home.

Ram a boy of 15-year-old; living with his parents who always fight with each other, as a result the boy is neglected. In order to get their attention he steals money from home and buys cigarettes and smokes, with his friends. His friends give company and support him as he brings money. The gangs encourage him to get into drugs and alcohol. Whenever Ram is at home he watches only the quarrel among his parents. So, he avoids staying at home.

What do you infer from the behaviours of Latha, Jeeva and Ram? Do you feel that their behaviours are different from normal children you observe? How are they different? What shall we do about these children to make them normal?

This is what you will learn in this lesson; understand your responsibility as a citizen who lives with these types of children with Behavioural Disorders (BD) and Emotional Disturbances (ED).

Learning Objectives

After reading this chapter the reader should be able to:

- Define the terms—Emotional disturbances, Behavioural disorders.
- Distinguish a child with behavioural disorder from a normal child.
- List the characteristics of the children with behavioural disorders and emotional disturbance.
- Suggest the remedial measures and to tackle the situations to combat the behaviour disorders and emotional disturbances.
- Discuss the need for arranging a suitable atmosphere both at home and school.
- Understand the role of the society in taking care/rehabilitation of these children.
- Analyse the causes of behavioural disorders and emotional disturbances.
- Understand how will these disturbances in the childhood will affect the child's life in future and prepare the remedial programmes accordingly.

Meaning and Definition

It is important to realise that all of us have gone through in our life periods of behavioural problems or emotional disturbance. Each one of us might have exhibited and experienced these behaviour in different forms. But by growing and understanding the world around us we might have changed over behaviours to suit the demands of our family and the society. But there are a few who continue to be exhibiting these behaviour problems/emotional disturbance and the parents, friends, teachers and others in the society find it difficult to deal with such people. A prolonged effort with consistency only will be a remedial measure to tackle these children.

It is estimated that about 10 to 20 per cent of children worldwide have such behavioural problems and it is chronic in them that interfere with their learning and adjustment in the society.

IDEA defines the BD/ED as under:

The term BE/ED means a condition exhibiting one or more of the following characteristics displaying over a long time and to a marked degree that adversely affect the child educational performance and the adjustment with others. They are surely mal-adjusted.

Characteristics of BD/ED

(a) Inability to learn that cannot be explained by any other factors such as intellectual, sensory or health.
(b) Inability to adjust with peers, teachers and others that lead to social defects.
(c) Inappropriate behaviour or feelings under normal conditions, like lying, cheating and steeling.
(d) Displaying of unhappiness or depression and irresponsible.
(e) Exhibiting physical problems such as aggressive, distraction, tempers, out blurting, fighting true week.
(f) They are anti-social destructor and aggressive.
(g) Emotionally disturbed, behaviourly disordered, socially adjusted, personally handicapped, conflicted and impaired.
(h) Children with BD/AD also have attention difficulty hyperactive disorder—AD/HD.

The term conduct disorder also refers to children who become aggressive and commit anti-social behavioural acts. They also display non-complaint behaviour. These behavioural lead to failures in schools/learning negative behaviours and mal-adjustment in adult hood. Behaviours disorders/Emotional Disturbance is classified as externalizing and internalizing behaviours and Teachers related adjustment and peer related adjustment.

Teachers related adjustment refers to meeting the behavioural demands and explicators of teachers for example they may externalize their behaviour through acting out, non-complaint defiance, low achievement, disturbing the class room ecology, resistance to social influence etc, and may internalize by exhibiting high level of appropriate class room behaviour, non-aggressive behaviour pattern problems with self and performance achievements.

Peer related adjustment refers to those skills needed to adjust with peer group and interact with them successfully when they move in a free atmosphere. Under externalizing behaviour patterns with peer related they may exhibited some acceptance, semen rejection, identity or failure to use social skills in establishing positive peer interactions high levels of social engagement and high level of negative/aggressive social behaviour. Under internalizing behaviour pattern we could observe the following. Neglected or rejected peer status, low level of participation in peer controlled achieves social isolation and withdrawal and low levels of negative social behaviour.

In old age BD/AD leads to depressions, which is also known as unpolar, and schizophrenia (a long term mental disorder). In a common mental illness, we discern that there is sadness, loss of interest in activities, decreased energy and recurring feelings of despair. During adolescence these behaviours lead to juvenile delinquency and anti-social behaviour. This is also related to learning difficulties in both boys and girls.

The children with BD/AD also act silly and act like clowns. Children who feel negatively about themselves act like clowns to seek the attention of others. Here peer influence is very powerful. They provoke the silly, foolish and clowny behaviours of positive or negative reactions from influential persons like peer group, parcuts, respectable adults and others can enforce clowning in the children who are lonely and disparate for attention. They learn this is the only way to get the attention of others in the society and continue to behave like this.

Children's behaviour is usually determined by how they feel about themselves. Feeling worthless, lacking in self-respect or lack of self-confidence influence. Their behaviour pattern, they have low self-esteem, over protected children does not learn to cope with everyday situations. They are afraid of taking any discussion as they feel that they might commit mistakes. They feel vulnerable, sensitive and incapable of fending for themselves. There may be social withdrawal of there children.

Children, especially when they are in adolescent stage engage themselves in anti-social and aggressive behaviours. They run away from home, indulge in truancy and commit unlawful acts. They may use alcohol or drugs that might lead to residential treatment.

Causes of BD/ED

Causes of behaviour disorder (BD) and emotional disturbances (ED) are of biological, social, educational, psychological, organizational, economic or political or combination of one or two of these factors. Where it is biological they indulge in physical injury or exposure to taxing leading to at risk behaviours. Mental depression has a biological basis, as extremely stressful events can trigger diforessive episodes. Genetic, neurological and body chemistry are closely associated with mental depressions. Similarly, drugs and loss of affectionate people will also lead to depressions.

Psycho-social Factors or Environmental Factors

Family, school, peer group and the social environment are the main components of psycho-social factors. When we talk about family as a factor, which causes behaviour/emotional disorders, it is meant economic condition—rich or poor, size of the family—small or large, relationship between father and mother, whether they are alike to provide on affectionate and conduct, supportive atmosphere at home, child abuse etc. If a child has a protected, happy atmosphere at home it will be well adjusted. If the conditions are negative it will lead to BD/ED. Abused child will have poor self-concept, poor impulse control and are frequently angry and aggressive.

School has a direct learning on the behaviour pattern of a child. Poor atmosphere will lead to a poor adjustment of a child. If a teacher is insensitive to students individuality and lacks pleasing behaviour, expects too much from them, when there is inconsistency in the behaviour of the management system, make the students to be more problematic and poorly adjusted to the school leading to poor result in the academic work and poor self-esteem. Similarly, when the curriculum is non-functional and irrelevant skills are taught it leads to BD/ED, as this type of atmosphere do not satisfy the childs requirements. Teachers also play vital role in the emotional, social, behavioural status of children. They can also be responsible for aggravating the behaviour problems by reinforcing inappropriate behaviours and ignoring appropriate behaviours which put great pressure on the child, the develop relative and poor self-concept.

Society also plays very important role in shaping the behaviours of children. Improvised environment including poor militron, disturbed family lead to sense of frustrations, hopelessness and aggressive behaviour. If the children and youth are not rewarded properly they try to get the attention of the society through anti-social behaviours, through crime, gang membership and other inappropriate behaviour.

Education of Children with BD/ED

Very little attention is being paid to provide appropriate education to children in the school who have behaviour disorders and emotional disturbance, as they are not identified properly at right time. There is less attention paid except punishing those children who exhibit the behaviour problems. Once it is identified that a child has the behaviour disorder and emotional disturbance to them. Parents have to seek juvenile homes where there is a regarces disciplining procedure. Sometimes this type of disciplining may agravates the behaviour problems.

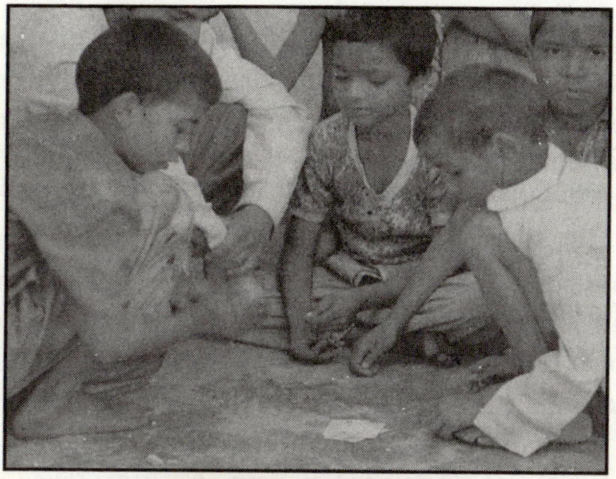

Delinquent Boys

Delinquent Girls

Playing Truency

A good education system for BD/ED children will first establish clear goals and expectations, provide varied opportunities to participate actively during instruction, closely monitor the progress of each learner, get feedback, and continuously evaluate the student's progress, especially the skills in which they have to have the mastery. Teachers should have clear goals of their instruction; follow multiple methods if instruction involving the students in learning-peer lutes ring, co-operative learning, choral responsibility in the class and more activities to let their energy to be released. Learning should be according to the choice of the child and the instruction should build on their strength and interest to create a motivating reward system. Activity leased curriculum and instruction will create interest and motive in these children.

Rehabilitation and Care

It becomes the responsibility of the family, community, and the medical people to recognize the problems of children with BD/ ED and provide early medical care and treatment, psychological support and hospitalisation if needed, society should participate family should protect, provide needed care and services, teach the skill needed for social adjustment, ensure family cohesive and network with families for their support in crisis. All these will help the children to have their rehabilitation by providing social support, education, vocational support, daycare service, long term care of needed and satisfy the spritual needs. Other sectors such as labours, welfare and law could help to provide quality care and service to these who are mentally disturbed. Care must be taken that everyone with BD/ED are cared and provided with at least one vocational skill so that they could earn their livelihood without depending on others and a burden to the society. It is the responsibility of every individual. If we fail to act, it will reflect the lack of our commitment to address the problems of children with behavioural disorder and emotional disturbances. We should dispel long held dogmas and shamus about the people with BD/ ED. So that they could have equal opportunities to participate in making their life happy and contribute to the nation building programmes.

Review Questions

- Who is called as BD/ED? Why?
- How does a child with BD/ED differ from a normal child?
- Explain the characteristics of children with BD/ED.
- When a child is hyperactive at home how will you handle?
- When a student refuses to participate in-group activities how will you encourage him/her to participate?
- How can different agencies help in rehabilitation programme?
- List the causes of BD/ED.
- How will you convince parents of children with BD/ED to accept them?
- Analyse your role in providing support to comb at the problems of the children with BD/ED.

11

Rehabilitation Services

Persons with disability do not ask for compassion but for an intelligent appreciation of their problems. They do not ask for charity but for opportunity. They need equal opportunity to participate in all walks of life without depending on others. We have to create the opportunities and a disable friendly environment to encourage them to feel like other normal people of their age.

Rehabilitation

Rehabilitation of disabled is a comprehensive and an almost all embracing process. It aims at providing health care services, social services, education and vocation to the disabled of all types, so that they can find the opportunities for developing and promoting their other innate talents and residual functions in order to make them function as normal members of the society. This is a complex and gigantic task calling for the collaboration and co-operation of experts in many disciplines, administrators, employers and the public at large.

Rehabilitation of the Planning and Execution

Rehabilitation is an inclusive programme where we try to provide proper and adequate health care services in order to arrest further expansion of the disability. They need day-care services to train them for independent living and to remove the stigma attached to disabled in the society.

On reading this package the reader should be able to:

- Define and explain what is rehabilitation?
- Identify the components of rehabilitation programme.
- Understand the objectives of rehabilitation programme.
- List the types of rehabilitation programme available.
- Develop awareness on the role of various voluntary agencies in rehabilitation of disabled persons.
- Develop the competency to assess the various programmes provided by government and non-governmental agencies.

We observe on the road many disabled people left uncared for and made fun of by the people. They may be of physically challenged, mentally challenged or with multiple disabilities. Their parents neglect them; and same parents disown them. We forget that they too have equal rights to live in this world like their normal counterparts. But on the contrary these people suffer. We must remember that disabled also have equal right to full participation in the nation building activities and affairs of life as the normal people. Aim of any welfare measure for disabled is to train them for independent living, to provide remunerative employment with an ultimate goal of integrating them with the community as well as make them adjusted and contributing members of the community. They should find a job in Sheltered Employment, Open Employment or should have Self Employment-independent occupations. So the ultimate aim of rehabilitation could be achieved only through right placement not only in an occupation but also in the society.

Rights of Disabled

They have the right to get educated like others, get free equipment, concession in the employment, comprehensive education programme according to the abilities of the disabilities should be prepared and all the possible help is to be provided.

On competition of general education, either in an inclusive school or special school, there should be provision for vocational education depending on the type or degree of disability, these should be for the development of their skills. A disable friendly campus should be ensured.

Special counters in the regular employment exchange or special employment exchange are to be opened, so that they could register for employment without much difficulty. There should be provision of reservation for disabled in all the sectors, at least up to 5 per cent.

We must ensure that they get appropriate transport facility for easy mobility to the educational institutions, place of work and to other place to make their living independently.

It is advisable that insurance schemes are introduced to the disabled persons also. The Government and the voluntary agencies should come forward to guide the disabled in this regard also.

All those who are involved in rehabilitation programme should identify appropriate and suitable trades in which disabled to be trained and placed.

Difficulties in Identifying the Disabled

People with disabled children have hesitation to reveal that they have a child with some disability. Even when surveys are conducted by any agency other then government or non-government, parents hide the fact. Sometimes such type of children are orphaned by being left in the hospital itself or throw out in the dustbin, or in the street. If they are noticed by the police or some agencies there is likelihood of their safety and care. Even when the government assures of some entitlement the surveys are not effective.

When some children are identified with some disability due to lack of provision for diagnosis the degree of disability is not diagnosed properly. In turn wrong or improper diagnoses lead to complication. This is also one of the reasons for parents not revealing the fact to others.

If care and protection is ensured by establishing guidance and counselling centres people will come out with the information about the children with disability, in their homes, or neighbourhood. Counselling centres should give assurance that they will keep it confidence and provide all possible help for their care, education, employment and rehabilitation. Assurance should be given that children with disabilities will not be neglected, cheated and condemned. Social activists should come forward to create awareness and ensure all these to the people.

The Government should establish in the primary health centres (PHCs) and hospitals a unit to diagonise and identify the disabled and provide adequate and proper health care services to them. This will create confidence in them. If there is severe degree of disability they should be admitted to special school or service centres. If the disability is moderate parents are to be advised to normal school.

Through its Education for All programme (Sarva Siksha Abhiyan) Government has taken initiative to train the primary school teachers as to how the disabled to be educated in the general classrooms along with the normal children. This provision is a great boon to children and relief to parents with disabled children.

NGOs and Rehabilitation

A band of revolutionary social workers who realized the urgency and the growing need of education and employment of the disabled started their own voluntary agencies to provide the needed services to them. Many NGOs also have come forward to provide care and education to disabled children. They work for the disabled with speech disorder, visual impairment, hearing impairment, emotionally disturbed and socially disadvantaged, physically challenged and mentally challenged, by providing day care services, educational facilities, prevocational training, vocational training, mobility training, awareness programme and wherever and for whomever rehabilitation is needed shelter is also ensured. The Government through Disability Commission in various states and Union territories assist these NGOs.

Wheel chairs, calipers and walking sticks for physically challenged, hearing aid with solar battery for hearing impaired, cooling glasses, Braille watches and the sticks to the blind, artificial limbs to those who have lost their legs either in accident or amputed due to diseases; health care services like surgery for those who are affected by polio, cleft palate etc. are provided by the Government through social welfare and rehabilitation centres.

Special scholarships are given to children with disabilities at the school level and for their higher education. If a normal person marries a disabled person like visually impaired, hearing impaired or physically challenged, special assistance upto Rs. 10,000 is given to them as a special recognition as it will help them to find a decent place in the society.

If any disabled wants to be self-employed they get loans from Bank and National Commission for Disabled, to enable them to be independent and contribute to the national income. The disabled can feel and prove to be a valuable human resource if they are given adequate opportunities for employment.

Travel concession is given to the disabled to travel by the Government transports to go to places like schools and colleges for study or going to the places for jobs or going to the hospitals for treatment.

Rehabilitation Commission runs in various places through State and District units special schools for visually impaired, hearing impaired, physically impaired and mentally challenged. Every district has a District Rehabilitation Officer to implement, take care of all these activities and monitor at the District level and a separate Directorate at the State level co-ordinates all the District level rehabilitation activities and coordinate with National Commission.

We can feel that we have done something to the disabled only when all the differently abled get a feeling that they have overcome their disability and have victory over their disabilities.

Review Questions

1. What is rehabilitation?
2. Who needs rehabilitation?
3. Suggest rehabilitation programme to be provided to the visually impaired.
4. What should be the components of rehabilitation programme?
5. Describe the role played by National Commission for rehabilitation.
6. When you find some disabled in your neighbourhood what action will you take?

References

Ann P. Turnbull *et al.* (1995) *Exceptional Lives-Special Education in To-day's Schools*, Englewood Cliffs New Jersey. Merrill, An Imprint of Prentice Hall.

Anna Nickson and Kevin D. (1997). *Identifying and Assisting Children with Behavioural Problems.* www yahoo.com

Bhargava, Mahesh (1994): *Introduction to Exceptional Children: Their Educational Provisions.* New Delhi: Sterling Publishers Private Limited.

Chauhan, S.S. (1989): *Educational of Exceptional Children.* Indus Publishing Company: New Delhi.

Deborah Deutsch Smith and Ruth Luckasson (1995) *Introduction to Special Education. Teaching in an Age of Challenge.* Allyn and Bacon. Boston.

Grace J. Craig and Marguerite D. Kermis. (1995) *Children Today.* Prentice Hall, New Jersey.

John P. Dworetzky (1990) *Introduction to Child Development.* (4th Edn.) West Publishing Company, New York.

Kar, Chintamani (1992): *Exceptional Children: Their Psychology and Education,* New Delhi: Sterling Publishers Private Limited.

Katrin Eun-Myo Park. (2006) *Health Watch: Up to One Fifth of the World Children Have Behavioural Problems.* Chronicle. UN. Online Edition.

Laura E. Berk. (1996) *Infants, Children and Adolescents.* Allyn and Bacon, Boston.

Mangal, S.K. (1993): *Advanced Educational Psychology.* New Delhi: Prentice-Hall of India Private Limited.

Pankajam, G. (2006): *Pre-primary Education: Philosophy and Practice.* Concept Publishing Company, New Delhi.

———(2006). *Know Your Child.* Concept Publishing Company, New Delhi.

Tom E.C. Smith *et al.* (1995): *Teaching Children with Special Needs in Inclusive Settings.* Allyn and Bacon, Boston.

Index

Ability Grouping, 94-95
Abnormalities, 121
Abraham Lincoln, 123
Abused Child, 148
Acceleration, 94, 96
Administrative arrangements, 94-95
Alteration Deficit Disorder, 107
Alternative schooling, 23
American Association on Mental Deficiency, 67
Anti-social activities, 132
Army Alpha Test, 92
Association for Children with Learning Disabilities, 105
Attention Deficit Hyperactivity Disorder (ADHD), 107
Auditory perceptional problem, 115
Autism, 118-122
  causes of, 120-21
  methodology, 121-22
Autism Spectrum Disorder (ASD), 120
Autistic children, 120-21

Backward children, 134-39
  characteristics of, 139-40
  causes of, 134-35
  education of, 139, 148-49
Barton Hall, 133
Behavioural disorders, 143-50
  causes of, 147-48
  characteristics of, 145-46
  education of children, 148-49
  meaning and definition of, 144-45
Behaviour intervention programme, 121
Berg, Fredrick, S., 55
Binot, Alfred, 88-89, 91
Blindness, 38-39
  causes of, 41
Boundary breaking activities, 98
Braille equipment, 23
  types of, 42
Braille Books, 47
Brainstorming, 130
Burt, 133

Cerebral palsies, types of, 27-28
Challenges, 17
Chicago-Non-Verbal Test, 92
Child care services, 122
Children, autistic behaviour in, 120
  educational backwardness, 132-38
  educational performances, 119, 145
  learning disability, 107
Children with special needs, abilities of, 20
  education and care of, 19-20
  solve/combet problems of, 18-19
Classroom arrangements, 47-48
Communication skills, 21
Community based rehabilitation, 23
Competition, 153
Comprehensive education programme, 153
Computer Assisted Learning (CAL), 121
Congenital ampulations, 29
Creative child, 123-30
  characteristics of, 124-25
  education of, 128-29
Creative expression, atmosphere of, 129
Creative potential, identification of, 125
Creativity, 123-28
  definitions of, 123-24
  development of, 127
  problems of, 127-28
Creativity tests, 125-27
Crippled children, 25, 34
Crisis management, 122
Criterion Referenced Tests (CRT), 113
Curriculum, 53, 79-80
  proper organization of, 130
Curriculum Transaction, strategies of, 81-82

Dehaan, 124
Dependent Mentally Challenged, 78-79
  principles of, 78
Depression, 146
Developmental disability, 119
Diagnostic test, 137-38
Differently abled children, 17-18
Direct Daily Measuring Device (DDMD), 113

Disabilities, 15-16, 20-25
Disabled children, 20-22, 155-58
  approaches of, 23-24
  difficulties in identifying, 154-55
  rehabilitation of, 152-53
Disability Commission, 155
Diseases, 25
Distance Learning, 23
Drevdahl, 123

Educating Mentally Challenged, 77-80
Education-curriculum, individualization of, 121
Education for All Programme, 155
Education approach, 22
Educational backwardness, 132-142
  causes of, 134-35
  problems of, 136
Educational opportunity, equality of, 30
Educational practices, 94
Educational procedures, 85, 121
Educational programmes, 16
Educational provisions, 30-36, 52-53
Effective special education programme, 23-24
Einstein, 123
Emotional disturbances, 143-50
  causes of, 147-48
  characteristics of, 145-46
  definitions of, 144-45
  education with children, 148-49
Employment exchanges, 154
Encounter Lesson, 98
Enrichment, 94
  programme, common approaches of, 96-97
Environmental causes, 135-36
Environmental factors, 147-48
Excessive day-dreaming, 128

Faulty emotional development, 134
Fletcher, Samuel G., 55
Fostering creativity, techniques of, 130
Frustration, 148

General education system, 22
General Mental ability, 92
Gifted children, 85-86
  administrative arrangement for, 94-95
  behaviour characteristics of, 89-90, 93
  educational practices, 94-95
  helping, 101
  identification of, 90-91
  problems of, 100-101
  teaching strategies of, 94, 97-98
  variations of, 94-95
Giftedness, causes of, 87-88
  characteristics of, 89-90
Group Non-verbal Intelligence Tests, 92-93

Guidance services, provision of, 142
Guilford, 87, 124

Hallahan, 112
Handicap, types of, 28-29
Harrington, 124
Havinghurst, R.J., 86, 124
Hearing impairment, 55-64
  causes of, 59-60
  characteristics of, 60-61
  definition of, 55-59
  educational provisions for, 62-64
  identification of, 61-62
Home based education, 23, 122
Home environment, 135
Home instruction, 34
Homi Bhabha, 123
Hospitalization, 18

Inclusive education with normal children, 22
Individual with Disabilities Education Act (IDEA), 20, 25, 50, 119
Individual Non-verbal Tests, 91-92
Individual Verbal Tests, 91
Informed Reading Inventories (IRI), 113
Insurance scheme, 154
Integrated education, 94
Intellectually gifted, 85
Intelligence Quotient, 88
Intelligence Tests, 137

Jalata, S., 92
Jon Eielson, 50
John White, 86
Johnson, 105

Karwoski, 123
Kaufman, 112
Kirk, 104
Kulu, Samuel, A., 16

Language Learning Association, 50
Language Tests, 91
Learning difficulties, classroom behaviour, 108
  definitions of, 104
  symptoms of, 106-07
  types of, 106-07
Learning disabled children, educational provisions for, 116-17
  identification of, 112-13
  special educational programme, 116-17
Learning disabilities, 103-117
  causes of, 110-11
  physical sign of, 107-08
  types of, 114-15
Learning Disabilities Act, 105
Learning objectives, 19-20, 26-27
Lesson, obectivities of, 119-20

Mahatma Gandhi, 123
Mental Age and IQ, concept of, 88-89
Mental retardation, 67, 134
  causes of, 72-74
  characteristics of, 75-77
  factors, of, 72-74
Mentally Challenged Children, 17
  causes of, 72-73, 77-80
  classification of, 68-69
  definition of, 67
  identification of, 73-78
  physical characteristics of, 68-69
Minimum Visual Tasks, 46
Multiple disabilities, 15
Mykblebust, 105

National Joint Committee on Learning Disabilities (NJCLD), 105
Newton, 123
Non-Governmental Organizations (NGOs), 112-13
Non-Test Techniques, 90, 93

Occupations, 19, 153
Open employment, 153
Organic disorders, 50
Orphans, 132, 143
Orthopaedic/physical disabilities, 27-28
Orthopaedically handicapped, 27, 30-31

Parents and Teachers, attitudes of, 46-47
Persons with Disability Act, 21
Phyllis Strums, 99
Physical and health disabilities, 134-35
  causes and prevention of, 28-29
  problems of, 26
Picture Completion Test, 92
Picture Construction Test, 126
Postural defects, 29-30
Pre-natal causes, 28-29
Psychological Tests, 138
Psycho-social factors, 147-48

Raven's Progressive Matrices Test, 92
Rehabilitation, 19-20, 151-52, 155-56
  programmes, 153
Rehabilitation Commission, 156
Rehabilitation services, 152-156
Rice, C.H., 91
Rights for disabled, 153-54

Sarva Siksha Abhiyan, 155
Schiyophrema, 120
Schonell, 133
Scholastic Achievement Test, 113
School environment, 135-36
Self-awareness activities, 98
Self-care activities, 82
Self-care programmes, 74
Self-employment, 153
Sensory disabilities, 37-64
  education provisions, 52-53
Shakespeare, W., 123
Sheltered employment, 153
Social adjustment, problems of, 45-46
Social characteristics, 16
Speech impairement, 49-50
  causes of, 51-52
  problems of, 52-53
Speech Therapy, 53-54
Speech education, future of, 21-22
Special education programme, 19-20, 79-80
  components of, 24-25
  purpose of, 20-21
  provisions, 139-40
Specific Learning difficulties, 109-110
Special schools and classes, 35
Stagger, 123
Standardized Achievement Tests, 137

Teacher's Judgement, 90
Teaching models, 131
Test-Techniques, 90
Trainable Mentally challenged, education of, 81-82
Trauancy, 141-42

University of Florida, 98

Van Riper, 50
Verbal Tests, 91
Visual perceptual problems, 115
Visually impaired, 39-40
  causes of, 41-42
  characteristics and problems of, 42-43
  classification of, 39-40
  identification of, 40-41
  prevention of, 48-49
Vocational education, 23
Vocational training and rehabilitation, 16

William Stern, 88
World War I, 92

Zero rejection policy, 23